GRAVE GOODS

For Catherine Luree
and the Bears

CONTENTS

The author wishes to thank and acknowledge the editors and publishers who first put many of these pieces into print: John Algeo at *The Quest*, William O'Sullivan at *Common Boundary*, David Robertson at the Putah-Cache Bioregion Project, Scott Slovic at *ISLE*, David Rothenberg at *Terra Nova* and the *Trumpeter*, and Dawn Marano at the University of Utah Press.

Grave Goods: Objects placed with the deceased on burial. They may represent the personal possessions, offerings to the dead man's spirit, or provisions for the spirit in, or on its journey to, the afterlife.
—*Dictionary of Archaeology* (Penguin)

Let us not be surprised that things so deeply hidden are dug out so slowly.
—Seneca

GRAVE GOODS

this

this
is what you love
the old she said

waving
bloody moonrag
close

yes

the butterfly
floating, hanging
on the wing

flaring, touching
down on the folding
earth

yes

suddenly

a lion
roaming
morning nothing mist

so

wet
in evening rain

yes

sets

this house
on fire
      —Gus Kenny, 1941

DREAMS OF VIRGINIA DARE

I WAS THERE THE NIGHT IT ALL BEGAN, BUT THE GREATER PART OF THIS story I've had to piece together over the years from reports of others, mostly friends of mine, who are usually pretty honest. It's customary in these situations to start by saying something like, "Verily, this tale is true." At least that's how all the old books begin. They claim that the power of enchantment—whether a magical charm, or an eloquent poem, or a good story told around the table—is so great that it is able to overwhelm all of nature. I don't know about that, but just try saying "I love you" to someone for the first time and see how the world is changed, for good or ill.

Nostalgia too must be something like this. After a couple of decades, people look back on their college years and say, "That was a magical time." Those folks are speaking figuratively and from a distance. What I'm trying to do is figure *out* some things, and thereby draw a little closer to the offbeat phenomena of the world, which, if they aren't magic in a literal sense are without a doubt "wicked," as they say in Maine, "wicked weird."

It was a college bull session. First day back for the fall semester and everybody was excited because there was a big football game the next day to kick off the new school year. A bunch of people were sitting around in the dorm lounge introducing themselves to each other or catching up on the summer's news with old friends. Among them was a new guy named Leo LaHapp, a freshman, who was on the cross-country team. Talk got around to the courses people were taking, and a couple said they were enrolled in Early American History. So Barb Taylor asked, "Does anybody remember Virginia Dare? I just love that name."

Virginia Dare, you may recall, was the first child born of English parents in the new world: August 18, 1587, on Roanoke Island in North Carolina. Not a good place to be from, all things considered, since not long after her birth everybody there disappeared without a trace. A few years later, when a long-delayed supply ship finally showed up from England, all they found were abandoned buildings overgrown with vines and a single word carved into a tree: *Croatoan*. Nobody knew what it meant, and there were no further signs of what happened to those unfortunate souls. All of them, including the baby Virginia Dare, were gone, never to be heard from again.

We were in Maine, so North Carolina seemed a pretty exotic topic—warm weather, sunny beaches, spring breaks—and it gave rise that evening to all kinds of fantastic speculations and associations. Somebody said that he knew of a bar called Croatoan—he thought that was the name—but it was down in South Boston. Somebody else said he was going to start a rock band and call it Croatoan. He imagined that none of the members in this band would ever take the stage, and nobody would know what they look like; instead they'd play in some hidden location far removed from the audience and pipe in the music via speakers so it would all be very mysterious, and rumors could start that the band was really led by Jim Morrison, who hadn't died after all.

That's when Leo LaHapp spoke up. He wasn't called "the Bug-man" yet. It was the first time anybody there had heard from him, so he was given the floor, and he surprised us by going on at length. Not a person in the room could have anticipated the succession of events after that. I realize that those of you who were there at the University of Maine will remember some of the incidents I'm about to recall—especially the infamous "Witch-Hunt"—but so far as I know, the strange and disparate occurrences of those days have never been brought together in an adequate account. I don't make any great claims for my own story, but it must suffice until a more satisfactory version is put forth.

Anyway, Leo LaHapp launched into his story, telling the group—all of whom were strangers to him—that he had once been to Roanoke Island and had seen there a marble statue of Virginia Dare. It was sculpted in the nineteenth century by Maria Louise Lander, a friend of Nathaniel Hawthorne, and it was the most exquisite work of art he had ever seen. This statue was life-size, presenting Virginia Dare as a beautiful young woman, mostly naked, a detail Leo delivered with great relish. He described her as standing, scantily clad, in the midst of a fancy garden, with flowering trees and sweet-smelling shrubs all around. It was as if the baby Virginia Dare had somehow escaped from the ill-fated colony and had grown up and was now living in Eden or Arcadia or maybe, as Leo believed, Croatoan.

Then he spoke of a legend concerning this statue, how on certain nights of the year it comes to life and starts walking around. "If only it were so," Leo sighed. "Something like that is very hard to believe, I know, and I don't go for it myself, but she does come to me in my special dream."

That got a few snickers from the audience, but we all wanted to hear more about this special dream, so we encouraged him to continue.

"I'm at home and for some reason my family has this huge dead bear in the middle of the living room. It's stuffed like it came from the taxidermist, so I ask around but nobody can tell me why this bear is here. 'Who killed it?' I keep asking my father, but he just tells me to go ask my mother, but I can't find her anywhere. Next thing you know, a big tree starts growing out of the bear's head. It's huge and already very old, even though it just sprouted. As it rises up, I think it's going to break through the roof of the house, but when I look up, there is no roof—it's gone and everything's just night sky with stars blazing and the tree soaring up there so high it looks like its leaves are the stars. Then way up there I see a woman swinging on a swing. She's naked and her skin is shiny white like marble. It's Virginia Dare. But she's not a statue anymore; she's alive and she's swinging and smiling and waving down to me. She wants me to climb up the tree, but the trunk is so big I can't get my arms around it. There's no place to grab hold. I get all upset because I can't climb the tree and I won't be able to go up there and sit on the swing and swing back and forth among the starry leaves with Virginia Dare. It's really frustrating. But she keeps swinging and smiling and waving down, as if to urge me on, so I try once more. Then I wake up."

He finished his recitation by expressing the wistful hope that one day, if that statue of Virginia Dare really does come to life and go for walks, she might make the trip up to Maine and pay him a visit. "In the meantime," he concluded, "at least I have my special dream."

A couple of the women in the audience thought the story quite romantic, but mostly people just snickered some more and exchanged knowing looks or the cuckoo sign with each other. When some of the guys started teasing him about being in love with a chunk of rock, Leo just got up and left, insulted.

But the talking went on well into the night, moving away from Leo and his statue to related topics of magic potions and amulets. "Wouldn't it be fun," Westphal suggested, "to find some way to grant Leo his wish and have that statue stop by and give him a thrill?" More plotting and scheming followed. At last somebody—I think it was Crilly Fritz (a real name by the way)—said: "Let's go find the Magician!"

The Magician was the nickname of a guy whose real name was Forrest Woodroe, an otherwise lackluster accounting major save for one curious fact: he came from a part of Maine that, at the time I'm talking about, still had a vibrant folk tradition of magic. It was somewhere up near Solon or Carrabassett maybe. The joke around campus was that while other kids were growing up playing with dolls or chemistry sets, the Magician was concocting potions and working out incantations. The bookshelves in his dorm room were lined with volumes by Albert the Great, Cornelius Agrippa, and Giordano Bruno. Forrest regularly wrote cryptic letters to the college newspaper interpreting current events in light of the prophecies of Nostradamus, signing his bizarre messages with the pen name Nick Cusa. Guys like this show up every fall on college campuses all across America. What separated Forrest Woodroe, what kept him from being just another freshman goofball, was the fact that people actually witnessed him alter the course of the 1975 World Series. It happened the year before I got there, but here's what they say about it.

Going into the sixth game of the Series, the Red Sox are down three games to two against the Reds, playing at home in Fenway. Everybody in New England is barnacled to their TV screen. The game goes into extra innings. Now it's past midnight. Bottom of the twelfth and leading off for the Sox is Carlton Fisk. On Pat Darcy's second pitch—a low inside sinker—Fisk takes a mighty swipe. The ball goes soaring up in a meteoric arc toward the wall in left field. It's a crisis, a moment when the past has least hold on the present and the present has greatest hold on the future. The ball becomes a lifeboat with all of New England's hopes crammed into it, and it's drifting dangerously toward the foul line.

Fisk takes a tentative step down the line toward first; stops; watches. Time stops and watches too. That's when the guys watching the game in the dorm lounge notice Forrest is standing performing this strange rhythmic motion with his arms, waving to the right as if to urge the lifeboat to keep from running afoul. Each wave is joined with a hop, so he's waving as he's bouncing his way across the room. Everybody's seized with wonder looking at Forrest, when suddenly a loud "Hey, look!" rings out in the room. Eyes return to the TV screen, where Carlton Fisk is now doing the exact same thing as Forrest—waving his arms as he hops, in just the same fashion, even keeping exactly in sync. Three waves with three hops: whoosh, whoosh, whoosh. It is a very strange moment, and it's going on even still: Forrest Woodroe leading Carlton Fisk in this weird dance across 250 miles and all of eternity.

But everything changes when the lifeboat hits the yellow foul pole above the wall—"Fair ball!"—and becomes a game-winning home run. The day is saved and Carlton Fisk is a hero! And to those sitting in the lounge of York Hall at the University of Maine on this faraway October night, so is Forrest Woodroe.

Even though the Red Sox would go on the next day to drop the ball and lose the Series to the Reds, that sixth game—capped by Fisk's unforgettable performance—went down as the greatest in World Series history. And Forrest Woodroe, for his part, stepped into campus history and was known ever after as the Magician.

As for what went wrong with the Sox in that remaining game, the Magician had a role in that too. Much to everybody's dismay, he was unable to make it back from some unspecified business in time for the game. The guys were counting on his working the magic one more time. They were plenty mad when he didn't show. Somebody even suggested that they burn the Magician at the stake for his failure, but death threats are ordinary in the mouths of disappointed Red Sox fans. Just ask Bob Stanley.

Cooler heads, though, prevailed that night in Maine, especially once it was reasoned that if this guy can sway the course of a World Series game, there's no telling what he might do to anybody who tried to mess with him. No one was willing to take that chance. Indeed, there are those who say that the Magician was so indignant about even the mild rudeness he suffered from those Red Sox fans when he finally did show up that he put a hex on their team so they would never win another World Series. One can conclude only that this, combined with the Babe Ruth curse, adds up to some pretty potent hoodoo.

And so the Magician now enters this story about Leo LaHapp and the statue of Virginia Dare. I myself have no part in the rest of it, save for the gathering of details after the fact. I have to admit that I did play a small role in hatching the scheme that called for the Magician's services, and it was me who came up with the idea to carve *Croatoan* into the Hollow Tree, thinking it might work as a kind of navigation beacon for Virginia Dare—but I didn't think anybody would take it seriously. Come on, this was a bull session.

When those guys from the dorm lounge—including, among others, Crilly Fritz, Peter Snell, and a muscle-bound guy that everybody called "Animal"—went off looking for the Magician, I stayed behind, and so did Westphal. For a little while we sat around trying to impress the women by making fun of how gullible those nitwits were. But then I got tired and went off to bed, leaving Westphal still trying to impress the women.

What went down next at the Hollow Tree came to light just this past Christmas—Westphal filled me in. Turns out the Magician was perfectly willing to help those guys help Leo get his girl. Carving the word *Croatoan* into the Hollow Tree was a great idea, the Magician said, but to cast an effective love charm—especially if it involved animating a marble statue—*that* would require a more formal ritual, for which the presence of all these guys was required. They eagerly agreed to it.

So it must have been at that point the Magician went to his closet, grabbed the blue denim laundry bag and shook out a bunch of dirty clothes onto the floor. Then he gathered a few items from a drawer, stashed them into the bag in a big clatter, and the whole crew set off for the Hollow Tree.

The Hollow Tree was a beloved campus landmark, a huge old cottonwood on the long, sloping lawn above the Penobscot River. It was the biggest tree around, and some people even claimed it was the largest in the state of Maine. At the base of its immense trunk was a gaping hole, wide as a church door, that led into an immense, rotted-out interior. Inside was cozy as a chapel, with space vaulting upward into the dim rafters of the world, where statues of angels and Madonnas might lurk unseen in dark niches. There was room enough in there you could celebrate a mass if you wanted, or have a party, or— more intimately—bring a date and make out.

Most everybody who attended the university in those days sooner or later did. It was a rite of passage and widely held that if you didn't make out in the Hollow Tree at least once before graduation, you couldn't really call yourself a University of Maine alum. Over the decades, the aura of all those comings together inside the tree must have inhered into the very xylem and phloem of that venerable monarch; if tree rings were a record of lovers' trysts rather than years, then this cottonwood easily qualified as the oldest living thing on earth.

I like to imagine that when the Magician and his band of dorm rats showed up there in the wee hours of the night, a pair of terrified love-birds were flushed from cover, bolting out from the Hollow Tree as the truth sometimes does in the course of things. There they go, a couple of quail, bobbing as they weave, hopping and tripping as they tug up on jeans, open shirt and open blouse unfurling behind them in a ghostly flutter. They flee across the dark lawn toward still darker reaches in the distance, until their fantastic forms fade into the same stuff from which everything after midnight is made, two blurs in the blur of darkness.

The Magician and company now stood in front of the Hollow Tree. Preparations were made for the ritual. The Magician emptied out the clattering contents of the blue denim bag: a can of Sterno, a camping pot, a potholder, some matches, and another item, hard to see. The Magician instructed Crilly Fritz to go inside the tree and carve *Croatoan* somewhere in its heart. With gusto Crilly pulled out his pocketknife and vanished into the cottonwood.

11

By the time he emerged from his task, the Magician had things set up on the grass. The can of Sterno was going. The guys stood in a semicircle around the Magician. Using the potholder, he suspended the camping pot over the blue flame. He had begun his conjuring. I guess you could call it that.

All of the guys now went dropped-jawed, looking back and forth between what the Magician was doing and one another, or maybe they were just looking for the exit sign. The Magician's spell, performed in a tone of voice that seemed to rise directly out of a catacomb, went something like this:

> *Draw Virginia from the wild,*
> *Home, my song, draw Virginia home,*
> *Home to Leo, home, my song, and pray:*
> *These words I weave as Venus bands*
> *Will draw, draw Virginia home!*

Most people are discomfited by poetry in one way or another, and these guys were no exception. But they were thoroughly undone when the Magician started to lower into the camp pot a waxen figure—some say it was in the shape of an angel, others say it was a bear, and there is one report that insists it was just a handful of birthday candles—and proceeded with his incantation:

> *Draw Virginia from the wild,*
> *Home, my song, draw Virginia home.*
> *As Croatoan takes its hold*
> *Deep in the heart of this tree,*
> *Draw Virginia home, my song,*
> *Draw Virginia home.*
> *As this wax melts in one*
> *And the selfsame fire,*
> *Even so let Virginia melt,*
> *Melt with love for Leo—*
> *And to others' love let loose all hold*
> *And draw Virginia home!*

By no academic standard can this be called good verse. You won't find stuff like this in a *Norton Anthology*. But if a poem is measured by the effect it has in the world, then this one reversed the magnetic pole of reality.

First thing the guys hear after the Magician finishes is the growling. It erupts from somewhere deep inside the tree, then pounces out like a panther or a really mad Bigfoot. Everybody, including the Magician, goes lime white and starts trembling like an aspen grove. The Magician himself is the first one to break, taking off like a barn-sour rental horse. The rest of them are right on his tail.

Given what happened over the next few days, it's no wonder these guys fell into tacit agreement never to mention this episode again. The whole thing is embarrassing. Even today if you manage to track one of them down and ask about that night around the Hollow Tree and how it might have been connected to the "witch-hunt" that followed, they will deny any knowledge of the topic. It's the main reason the story didn't get out before this.

Here's the next part.

The other famous campus landmark was in front of the gym: a bigger-than-life-size statue of a black bear. The black bear is the University of Maine mascot, and this one had been around since the days of Rudy Vallee. I've seen a yellowed photo of old Rudy standing next to this bear. The singer is wearing a long raccoon coat and is crooning something through a megaphone, probably the "Maine Stein Song." So this picture would have to have been taken in the late twenties. Otherwise pretty ferocious looking, the bear was made out of wood and plaster, so by the time we got to college in the seventies he had been chewed up by termites and was looking pretty mangy.

On the very next morning after the high jinks around the Hollow Tree, Peter Snell was heading to the gym when he was shocked to discover the bear was gone! There was the empty pedestal, and all around it he could see footprints and deep ruts leading off in the direction of the woods. Peter Snell had flunked basic math a couple times, but this two-and-two he could put together. He ran back to the dorm terror stricken, with the whole pack of junkyard dogs that was his imagination nipping at his heels.

He found the rest of the Magician's assistants from the night before and warned them of the big trouble afoot. Whatever levelheadedness had remained among them had now been dropped into a vat of acid. Greg Downing, another dorm resident, happened to be walking past the room where they were in heated deliberation. What he overheard didn't make much sense, so he thought it was just another bunch of Saturday morning drunks. He wasn't able to say who said what, but among the fragments of conversation preserved in his report are these:

"Shit! Do you really think that bear's name was Croatoan?"

"Shit! Is *that* what we heard growling in the tree?"

"Shit, we gotta get that bear back—the football team's gonna kill us!"

And last: "That Magician is a dead man!"

Then the guys charged out of the room—no need to repeat their names, you know them by now—and went off, presumably to grab the Magician and force him to set matters aright. One of the things we learned in political science class was that the solution to the problems of democracy is more democracy; the same might be said, at least in this case, when it comes to folly.

Now, believing that a ratty old statue of a bear, some dilapidated university mascot, could be conjured—even by mistake—into life, and that its name would just happen to be Croatoan, is by no means as far-fetched as you may think. Wacky behavior stemming from wayward belief happens all the time in America. It may be the only story we've got.

Compare, for instance, the man from Plymouth, Massachusetts, who, a couple hundred years ago, had an idea about how to bring in a few more tourist dollars to his pretty how town. He went down to the harbor and walked out onto the strand of dreams. Or maybe it was a mudflat. The place was strewn with unremarkable boulders dropped there about ten thousand years ago—a heap of junk a glacier didn't want anymore. It had been lying there like this for millennia. But he walked around for a while, like people do in Fairly Reliable Bob's Used Car Lot, and at last selected a boulder, perhaps the least remarkable of them all, into which he chiseled four numerals: "1620." Next thing you know, the rock exploded into myth.

Historians assure us that the picture of Pilgrims stepping off the *Mayflower* onto this rock as if it were a welcome mat to the new world is little more than a charming bit of Thanksgiving lore, but it nevertheless translates into some overly firm belief. In 1835 Alexis de Tocqueville (that shrewd Frenchman) observed just how obsessed Americans had already become with this coffin-size piece of glacier trash: "I have seen fragments of this rock carefully preserved in several American cities, where they are venerated and tiny pieces distributed far and wide." Today Plymouth Rock is housed in a kind of Greek temple, and it draws millions of people a year to an otherwise unexceptional place surrounded by sour cranberry bogs, lonesome pine woods, and smelly salt marshes. Talk about conjuring!

Well, the guys did find the Magician that day, sometime around sunset, and hauled him back to the Hollow Tree, where they planned to make him cancel the faulty spell cast the night before. But when they got there a lot of angry people were swarming about on campus—the football team had just lost—and the Hollow Tree was in plain sight, so our boys beat a hasty detour to the forest behind the university and went down the woods path that the cross-country team trained on.

At some point they left the trail and pushed into the dark spruce and fir forest where they found hundreds of small cheesecloth bags festooned from nearly every branch of the evergreens. The guys thought this a little strange, but they had bigger and stranger worries: they had to get that bear back before somebody got hurt—namely, them—at the hands of a superstitious football team and its angry fans.

By the time they reached a spot secluded enough to perform whatever crazy ritual deemed proper by the Magician, dusk had settled in.

"Get going," Animal said as he gave the Magician a nasty shove. "Get that bear to go back where it belongs."

"Look," the Magician said, "I'm not sure I can. I don't know any spells that work on bears."

"What do you mean? Look what happened last night. Sure as hell looked like it worked to me. Just say the same thing, and make sure you mention the bear's name again."

"What are you talking about? What name?"

"Croatoan, you idiot!"

"I don't have my magic kit," the Magician said. "I left it at that tree last night. When I went back this morning to get it, all the stuff was gone."

"We don't have time for that crap. This is serious. Look, here's some candles. We'll light them and stand around holding them and you just sing that damn bear back to where the hell it goes. Now do it!"

Alas the Magician, wanting his bag of tricks, did the only thing any performer can do in such a situation—he winged it. Who knows exactly what words he chanted, but they came through in that same catacomb tone, only now they tumbled along through the dusky forest like empty trash cans in a Halloween wind.

Little is understood anymore about the relation between word and world. In sounding it out, you might think there is some vast separation between them, starting with the letter *L* and reaching out to every level of meaning. But this would be an error. There is no separation, or so they say. To the artists who work in this medium—which goes by the name of magic—there is a conviction that nothing happens by chance or luck. These people align their actions with some bigger principle, in some cases bright and shining, and in others very dark indeed. All of them use the human voice to express the inner nature of the mind, to draw forth its secret manifestations and to declare the will of the speaker or a guardian angel or whatever demon might have stowed away for the course of any particular human life.

Maybe, as you say, all of this is just a load of hooey. You wouldn't be wrong. But if it had been *you* jogging down the woods path that evening on your way back to the field house after a strenuous and solitary training run because you showed up late for cross-country practice, and you heard that creepy chanting coming from the dark woods and had seen the candlelight flickering among the somber spruce and fir boughs, then maybe *you* would have been struck as poor Leo LaHapp was struck that evening: with the firm impression that there was a coven of witches out there in the University Forest and they were conducting some dark ritual, probably a black mass.

"Holy shit!" you would say, picking up the pace and running the fastest mile you'd ever run in your whole life (and nobody there to see), just so you can get back to campus in time and sound the alarm: "There's witches out there—I mean it—and they're doing animal sacrifices and who knows what all! We gotta stop it!"

Yes, had all this actually happened to you, then a few pages in the underground history of the University of Maine would have been devoted to your exploits. That is, if anybody bothered to write it.

But this is Leo's story, and here's what happened to him.

He emerged from the forest and Paul-Revered it around campus, hustling from dorm to dorm shouting about witches. At first people just dismissed Leo as a rowdy or a drunk, but then he managed to convince a couple of resident assistants at the dorm to go into the woods with him to investigate.

Flashlights in hand, they retraced Leo's path. Along the way, they saw the cheesecloth bags hanging in the trees. Nobody knew what they meant, but agreed they looked pretty sinister, like little ghosts that had snagged themselves in the branches. Then they found some smoking candles lying in the forest duff. But what clinched it was when they heard, from deep in the recesses of the night woods, a horrible racket of breaking branches and snorting animals and demonic cursing, as if a bunch of people were running away. It sounded like a coven of witches!

There's no telling where in the human mind that switch is that, if thrown, turns on mob mentality, but Leo, groping around in there for anything to throw some light on his experience, managed on that memorable Friday night to trip it.

The whole campus lit up in a frenzy. It was like a kindergarten game of Telephone gone haywire, or an adult game that politicians used to play called the Domino Effect. Whatever it was, it was nuts and it was fast. As Westphal describes it: "Next thing you know there's two hundred guys with baseball bats and hockey sticks pouring out of the dorms and heading for the woods. God help anybody they found out there. I think they killed a couple of black cats, I'm not sure, but a lot of those guys were already drunk and pissed off that the football team had lost, so when they couldn't find any witches, they started beating each other up. That witch-hunt was the scariest thing I've ever seen, and it went on all weekend."

It was as though the campus had sent up a weather balloon into Cloud Cuckoo-land. It stayed up there for a day and a half. In the meantime, the Witch-Hunt was big news, and almost everybody was taking it seriously.

Since Leo was the first one to spot the trouble, he became a hero of sorts, as well as the de facto spokesman for what was going on. He was now the Cotton Mather of U Maine, demanding the purge of baneful influences. He thought people would be interested in what he had to say, so he set up a sort of press room in the dorm lounge.

At first it was just a single reporter from the campus newspaper, but as the scope of the events widened, press from off campus started showing up. In eastern Maine, any fuss is big news. Soon there were rumors that TV cameras were on their way and maybe Huntley and Brinkley too. Lucky for Leo, those who knew the real story, including the fine points of his special dream, had their own problems and were lying low.

With Leo at the helm, all kinds of fools started making reports. Stories came in about strange mounds of earth discovered out in the forest. "It must be where the witches buried their victims," exclaimed one sociology major on Sunday morning. For the rest of the day you saw guys heading off into the woods with shovels. Then came the psychology major who said he saw a bunch of naked people, obviously witches, darting among the trees. "And if you don't believe it, here's a shirt I found out there!" This sent even more people out into the woods; nobody wanted to miss out on a chance to lay hands on these witches. Finally, there were several UFO sightings that weekend, and one thoroughly besotted philosophy major claimed to have been abducted by the aliens, vicious beings who—he insisted— had robbed him of everything. "I can't even remember my name," he sobbed over and over to the reporters, as Leo stood there with a comforting arm around the poor scholar's shoulders. "We must recover this good man's name," Leo intoned for the record.

Monday morning was when that weather balloon came crashing down. It dropped in the form of a graduate student in forest entomology who came bursting into Leo's "press room" with a bug up his ass. He said he had been away for the weekend and just gotten back. He had this big experiment going for his dissertation research on spruce budworm. It involved setting up cheesecloth traps out in the forest to catch the insects. When he went out to the site this morning, he found all the traps had been ripped from the trees. Three years of research down the drain. Or up in smoke as the case may be, because he learned that students from one of the Christian organizations had pulled them down and burned them in a ritual bonfire out in the forestry school's "Stump Dump."

"They thought my traps had something to do with witchcraft!" the bewildered grad student declared, as reporters busily scribbled down notes. He also said something about finding a badly charred bear's head nearby. "What the hell's going on around here?" he demanded.

"Oh shit," said Leo, as he bolted out of there before the grad student could grab him or any TV cameras showed up.

Next day the campus newspaper headline read: "Witch Hunt Proves a Witch Hunt. Campus Bugged by False Report." Many humiliating details found their way into that story, but somehow Leo was spared public exposure of his special dream. At least he still had that. Also, there was no mention of the Magician, Crilly Fritz, Peter Snell, Animal, or any of those other mischief makers from the dorm.

Even today very few know about Virginia Dare's role in all this. For Leo's sake, I'm glad. I hope he forgives me for invoking her one more time, but I think these things can now be laid to rest. Everybody should know that the Witch-Hunt wasn't really Leo's fault; he was just caught up in a swirl of circumstances. Once that story broke, his reputation on campus was ruined. Nobody called him a hero after that. They didn't even call him Leo anymore. Instead, he was simply "the Bugman." And the Bugman he remains.

There's a mawkish pleasure one takes in calling to mind events such as these. Sometimes I think my college years were misspent in pulling pranks and cutting classes so I could sit around and write stories like this to entertain my friends. Then I comfort myself by thinking that nothing that happened back there, no matter how silly, was far removed from anything else going on in the world. It was the seventies, and everybody was doing this kind of thing. Call it the "spirit of the times." Every age has one.

"What a waste!" people say when I tell them the kinds of things we did in those days. "How did you ever make anything of your-selves?" Well, maybe it's like the millions of seeds a cottonwood tree flings out into the world each spring, those tiny, feathery parcels of hope that float together in the air for a while, just drifting around in companionable oblivion. Only one or two of them might ever come down to earth and find a nurturing spot to take root, someplace where they might indeed "make something of themselves."

After all, while we were sitting around a University of Maine dorm on that Friday evening a quarter century ago, concocting schemes to animate a statue and put a love spell on it, on the other side of the continent there were others with names like Jobs and Wozniak sitting around conjuring up a computer that would be named for a fruit that comes from a tree in Eden, a computer small enough and friendly enough that everybody in the world might own one, a magical box to be connected to millions of other boxes all over the world, so that in the end, no matter whatever else might be said of any individual, each would be a node in some infinite web, each an electric sparkle in the eye of Indra.

And thus my wayward college days are redeemed—because they were never lost in the first place, never removed from the center of things in this centerless universe. In fact, so far as this story goes, they *are* the center. It's mind-boggling to consider: whatever it is that causes one idea or name to gain purchase in the wider world while another fades away just may be what ultimately distinguishes a college prank from true magic. Or, as some are inclined to see it, history from myth.

In any case, you may be wondering how it came about that I should now have all these details. Perhaps you're curious as to what happened to the people who appeared in this sketch, or maybe you'd just like to check out these places for yourself, much as literary tourists do when they rummage around the Catskill Mountains looking for Rip Van Winkle's bed, or when they scour Wall Street trying to find the building Bartleby worked in. There's no going back to such places, except by the way we just came. But if you insist on historical accuracy, I'll do my best, though this particular bag of tricks is nearly empty.

First of all, the Magician. He did graduate from U Maine and went on to Harvard Law School. After that he got a job with some Big Eight accounting firm and got busted in the eighties for insider trading. Last I heard he's selling furniture in Farmington, Maine. The rest of those guys from the dorm I haven't seen or heard about in years, but with names like Crilly and Animal, you can be sure they are well known in their respective neighborhoods, wherever they may be. As for the Bugman, he dropped out of college after one semester, to chase his special dream elsewhere, maybe in Croatoan.

Speaking of Croatoan, for several years after these events, lovers and other visitors to the heart of the Hollow Tree were baffled by this odd word they found carved there. It became part of the campus folklore. There was even a story about a young couple who, not long after graduation, had a baby they named Croatoan, no doubt because she was conceived in the Hollow Tree.

Ah, the Hollow Tree. Sad to say, but even mythical giants must fall. Sometime after I left Maine, the Hollow Tree came down. I can only hope that it wasn't rudely toppled as if it were just another piece of timber sliced up into logs and hauled off for target practice in the Stump Dump, where junior lumberjacks fling axes at old carved hearts and one mysterious word—or worse, carted away to the Old Town mill and pulped into the paper you're reading this on. I would hate to think that this book is all that remains of a million "I love yous" and one special dream. Whatever, the Hollow Tree is gone from U Maine. I wonder if anybody there even remembers it anymore.

As for that old black bear mascot that disappeared—his name wasn't Croatoan. As far as I can determine, he never had a name. Nor did he ever stand up from his pedestal and stalk the campus. Turns out that on the Friday evening before the disappointing football game, the Alumni Association had held a little ceremony. The old bear was being retired. The president of the university said some gold-watch words, then a crane hoisted the crumbling bear onto a flatbed truck that carried it away and unceremoniously dropped it off in the Stump Dump, for lack of a better paddock. Given the mayhem of the next few days, it's not surprising that nobody ever asked about its mysterious disappearance from the Stump Dump. But there's an aging entomology grad student—still trying to repair the damage to his career after the disastrous spruce budworm experiments—who could tell you a thing or two about that bear's fate.

So if you had your heart set on seeing a bear at the University of Maine, don't fret—they replaced it. The new mascot is a bit smaller—

"leaner and meaner" as the Alumni Association likes to say—and it's made of cast bronze. Some say bronze was chosen so as to prevent the rotted-out destiny that overtook its predecessor. But there are a few—and you know their names—who believe that using heavy metal was the only way to ensure that if *this* mascot should ever come to life, its own weight would keep it from going anywhere. Thus this bear is now fixed in place more firmly than most treasured beliefs.

At long last, there is the mystery of the growl. As I said, I was able to pick up the threads of this story thanks to Westphal. I paid him a visit over Christmas down on Mount Desert Island, and we got to talking about our college days. The Witch-Hunt came up, as it sometimes does when we get together. This time he provided all of the details of the events at the Hollow Tree, and I wondered how he came upon this expanded version. I knew he hadn't gone along with the Magician and company that fateful night. I pressed him.

"So what gives?"

"Come on down in the cellar with me." He grinned impishly, an expression I know all too well.

Westphal lives in an old house. Cellars in these places are spooky. They're dimly lit and smell like the earth's dirty laundry. As he led me over to some dark shelves on a back wall, he said, "Hey, O'Grady—that growl? It was me. I beat those guys to the Hollow Tree and was hiding inside, up in one of those dark places you can't see from below. I scared the shit out of them—you should have seen it."

"No way!" I said.

"Well, then, how do you explain this?" He reached up to the highest shelf and brought down an old blue denim bag, clattering with stuff inside. He handed it over to me. We were a couple of bank robbers, and here was my share of the loot.

And that's all I got.

TELLING THE BEES

ONE SUMMER DAY SOME YEARS BACK A MAN SHOWED UP AT THE DOOR
seeking permission and something else. No ordinary caller, he was
dressed in full beekeeping gear: coveralls, high-top Redwing boots,
long coated gloves, and a thick veil of dark mesh that hung like an
ominous cloud from the broad brim of his white hat. In his left hand
he held an old tin bee smoker with noxious plumes curling from its
stack. What was he doing here? We had no bees.

Yet, he wasn't a total stranger, or so we told ourselves. Wasn't he
the man seen every week at the farmers' market, the one who sold
the raw honey and beeswax? He had a small table with a hand-
lettered sign on it that read "Locally produced." We never bought
anything from him, and didn't know anybody who had. Stories
around town hinted that his honey was tainted; his bees spent too
much time up in the mountain laurel and rhododendron that grew on
the mountains. Honey made from those flowers is said to contain a
toxin that, ingested in even small amounts, leaves you flat on your
back for a day or more, hallucinating. "Mad honey," the teenagers call
it. Not that we had anything against a sweet madness or weren't
willing to take a chance, but none of us cared for honey. We preferred
maple syrup.

Before we could ask what brought him to our door, he told us. It
had to do with a loss he suffered involving a particular beehive now

located in our woods, or in the woods just beyond our woods. So he said. We didn't know anything about any beehive. He assured us it was out there nonetheless, and it belonged to him.

He went on at length about the trouble that had arisen between this hive and himself. A falling out had occurred. About a year ago, the man's mother—whom he referred to as "the queen beekeeper"—had died. The next day the hive was empty, the bees having pulled the apiary equivalent of running away from home.

"They were upset with me," he explained. "You're supposed to tell the hive whenever there's a death in the house. They're sensitive, you know, and consider themselves part of the family. When Mother died, I just forgot to tell them. You can understand this, can't you? It was a sad and busy time, so many things to take care of. Mother's last request was that her coffin be filled with honey before we put it in the ground. Not an unusual desire for a lifelong beekeeper, so don't look at me like that.

"I went out to the hive and gathered all the honey they had in there, but it was hardly enough. I had to call around to every honey warehouse in the region until I finally had what I needed. It was difficult work and involved a lot of driving, not to mention the grieving I was doing—no wonder I forgot to tell the bees Mother had died. It's not like I was trying to hide anything from them or go out of my way to be rude. But the bees were peeved, and I don't know if they were offended because I didn't tell them about Mother or because I went out and got all that stranger-honey for her coffin. Whatever the reason, they abandoned me. It's terrible, and I've been looking for them ever since.

"I finally spotted one of them this morning and followed it up here. The hive must be nearby. I have to tell them I'm sorry. I just hope they forgive me and come home."

This entire story came to us through the dark mesh of his veil. Listening to it was like sitting on the priest's side of the confessional window. We wondered if he had been snacking on his own honeycomb.

"Look!" he exclaimed, pointing at something moving across our field toward the woods. "There goes another one now."

None of us could see anything where he was pointing. Maybe a dark veil makes it easier to see the hard-to-see things.

"Would you mind," he asked, "if I followed that bee into your woods and had a look around for the hive?"

We felt a certain sympathy for him based on his story, and his request provided a novel reason to get outside, so we said sure. We even offered to help look for his bees out in our woods, or in the woods just beyond our woods—we were willing to go that far.

"Thanks," he said. "Follow me." He darted for the forest and was immediately taken in by it.

We were only about a minute behind him, but it was already too late. The Catskill Mountains in summer are lush and fraught with obstacles to following even a man lumbering along in a beekeeper's suit. The leaves on the trees only serve to hide the immense lichen-shrouded boulders strewn everywhere. Trunks and leaves notwith-standing, those big rocks effectively hinder all lines of sight, so once the man stepped into the woods that was it. For a while we could hear the crashing of his progress up-slope through the dark trees and thick understory. Soon, though, it faded away. Before long we were lost.

Maybe that's all we were after anyway. We did this sort of thing many a time, and rather enjoyed the aimless gadding about that inevitably brought us out on some faraway and unfamiliar road, where we could hitch our way home. Since we possessed no maps or guide-books—save for a couple of antiquated and unreliable volumes ac-quired at flea markets—we came to know our region by employing more rash methods. Friendly faultfinders have often suggested that my writing and thinking are caught in a similar drift.

Anyhow, since it looked like our mission was turning into another one of those free and easy wanderings, one of us proposed we wait around until a bee flew by, then follow it to the hive and the man. Such a plan was a bit more systematic than was our wont, but we agreed to give it a try. We didn't have long to wait. And we didn't need a veil to see the bee. Keeping up with it, however, was another story.

We lost it almost immediately, but at least we now had a confident vector to follow. We were making what progress we could when another bee buzzed by, confirming our course. Then another, and another. We had merged into honeybee rush-hour traffic, and remained in it for a long time. Our beeline took us deeper into the woods and higher up on the mountain, but still no sign of the hive or its contrite keeper.

Just as we were about to give up hope of ever achieving our goal—and muttering that we didn't need the help of any bees to get ourselves lost in the woods—we came upon the tombstone. After that, we forgot all about the hive.

We were high in the mountains and far from the usual tombstone habitat. Up here you'd sooner expect to discover a bird-of-paradise in bloom. The marker itself was carved from native sandstone, and we found it toppled over, nearly buried in a few human lifetimes of fallen leaves. We might have walked right past it, had it not been for the partially obscured letters engraved at the top.

"Hey, that looks like a tombstone! What's it say?"

We brushed away the upper layers of detritus, exhuming a name: *Rip Van Winkle*.

"No way! This is a joke, right? He was just a character in a story."

"Well, who would make a tombstone for him, and why put it up here?"

"Think a body's underneath there?"

"I don't know. Let's dig some more."

With our hands, we removed further layers of forest debris, going down through the moldy horizons of soil that had begun to consume the stone. Our work smelled like old books.

Soon a graven image was revealed, just below Rip's name. It looked like a mountain lion—around here they're called panthers—surrounded by seven stars, or what looked like stars. Maybe they were bees. Hard to tell what they were because the stone was so timeworn and soiled. The panther also had something in the grip of its jaws, perhaps another star or a bee. We kept digging.

We were past the organic layers and into the mineral soil and unconsolidated glacial till. By this point we were using sticks for digging tools. As we labored away, an inscription began to emerge, scrolling up from the earth as we scratched our way deeper into it:

> *Just above, upon this crest,*
> *For twenty years Rip took a rest.*
> *Now he's gone where all men go . . .*

We had reached a point where the tombstone was broken off. The lower half with the remainder of the inscription was missing. We continued to dig, hoping to get to the bottom of it, but turned up nothing except more mineral soil and glacial till.

We were disappointed not to have the complete text of Rip Van Winkle's epitaph, but still we had this tantalizing fragment. In the years since, we've spent many a satisfying hour down at Pandora's Tavern discussing the questions the tombstone raised for us: Was this really Rip Van Winkle's grave? Was he a real person, and not just the offspring of an author's imagination? And if he was real, did he actually encounter that strange band of men in the wilderness, just as the story says?

You remember the story, don't you? Rip wanders off into the mountains with his dog one afternoon, ostensibly to do a little squirrel shooting, but really he's trying to get away from his workaday duties and the clamor of his wife. Back then they didn't have sports bars and golf courses and men's groups; instead, a man went squirrel shooting. After hiking along for many hours and occasionally discharging his firearm into the trees but never hitting anything, Rip runs into this crew of odd-looking men dressed in quaint and outlandish clothes. Apparently, they're having a party up here in the mountains—there's a keg of potent mead and everybody's playing at ninepins. Funny thing is, though these fellows are trying to whoop it up, none of them breaks a smile or even says a word. It's as if they can't decide whether to have a bachelor party or a funeral reception.

Rip is recruited to pour the mead into flagons and serve it to the somber revelers. He's happy to do so, and as a naturally thirsty soul helps himself to repeated draughts of the brew. Before long his senses are overpowered and his eyes are swimming in his head. Finally, he passes out—for twenty years.

When at long last he awakens from his slumbers with one of those what-did-I-do-last-night? headaches, there's no trace of the strange crew or his dog. In addition, his rifle is rusty, his beard is white, and his joints ache. If what the epitaph on the tombstone says is true, then we had come upon the very spot where the events in the story took place. Should the Park Service ever find out, they'd turn it into a National Historic Site, build a road up here, and put in a visitor center.

The problem is we were never again able to find that spot with its tombstone. On that long ago day, after many hours of roaming back down the mountain and through the forest, we finally broke out on a road. We were in an urgent haze of excitement. We couldn't wait to tell the world of our discovery. Rip Van Winkle's tombstone—think of what this could mean!

Well, what the world—at least our small part of it—thought was we were nuts. Either that or making the whole thing up. Especially when, a few days later, we led a group from the local historical society up the mountain in order to show them the tombstone. It's easy to lose your way up there. We couldn't locate the spot.

Matters weren't helped any when the next week, seeking corroboration, we went to the farmers' market looking for the man who sold the honey. He wasn't there, nor was he in the weeks following. Finally we asked around and were told he had moved away, taking his bees and mad honey with him. Now there was no way of knowing if he was even the one who showed up at our door that day. We never saw him again.

Events such as these certainly cast doubt on our impulsive methods of reckoning: the world demands proof, and all we have is our word. But if you'll take mine for it, I assure you that tombstone is out there. We *did* find it once, way back when we followed the beekeeper into the forest. I myself have continued to look for Rip Van Winkle's tombstone—often in the company of friends—but alas, no luck. My understanding companions, however, usually enjoy the hike, and all of them like the story.

Their favorite aspect of the tale, more often than not, concerns the last extant line of the epitaph: "Now he's gone where all men go . . ." People have always been intrigued by the question of where it is, exactly, that all men go. And for that matter, where do they come from? Whether pertaining to flesh-and-blood historical figures or mere fictional characters, questions of coming-into-being and passing-way remain vital.

A few weeks after our dismal performance with the historical society, a jar of honey showed up at our front door. A note attached to it read: "Thanks. Fred." Was it from the beekeeper? Did he actually locate the hive, tell the bees he was sorry, and bring them home? Was this his way of thanking us for our help? Even if that was so—and we never did find out for sure—none of us were willing to try that honey. Those bees had been living too long on their own up in the wild reaches of the mountains. Who knows what unfamiliar nectar they may have been sipping.

Or perhaps the jar left at our door was simply an accident. This Fred had made a mistake, confusing our place for that of someone to whom he owed a debt of honeyed gratitude. Or more likely, the whole thing was just a prank by one of the many skeptics we encountered in telling of our experience. No matter. Let's just say something like along these lines is what happened.

Thus our mysterious beekeeper—that veiled man on a quest for forgiveness—is still out there in the forest, high up in the Catskill Mountains. Like Rip Van Winkle, he ran into a strange crew of sourpuss men playing at ninepins and trying to have a party. He wound up serving as their bartender and helping himself to repeated draughts of their wicked mead. If that's the case, he ought to be waking up any day now.

A TREE OUT THERE

IT HAS BEEN SAID THAT EACH OF US HAS A TREE OUT THERE SOMEWHERE.
In former times it was customary—and in some places may still be—
to plant a tree for good luck when a baby is born. Thus one's tree
was right there in the yard, and it would grow with the child; between them they enjoyed an intimate rapport with life, a shared
destiny. This symbolic tree was carefully tended. If it flourished, so did
the human being; but if it was afflicted with blight or perished, the
corresponding human life suffered a fate in kind. There was an affinity
between the arboreal and human realms, expressed in a language
unbound by any dictionary. I have heard that if you know how to
"read" your tree, you have a most effective oracle. These days, however, you must first go out there and find it.

Prince Siddhartha searched many years before finding his tree, and
when he did he sat himself down in its shade and became the Buddha. Adam and Eve found their way to a tree—one of two that grew
in the Garden of Eden—the Tree of Knowledge of Good and Evil.
For reasons of his own, God had told the couple to stay away from it,
but they ignored the warning and ate of its fruit. God found them
out and was vexed; he banished them from the Garden before they
could get to the other tree. My friend Jan VanStavern found hers, a
venerable maple, growing in front of her childhood home. Upon
returning from school each day, she would throw her arms around it

in a great embrace. Today she measures the character of those who enter her life by hugging them: the noble souls feel like the old maple tree.

I caught a glimpse of my own tree once, when I was a boy growing up in New Jersey. It was an early morning in mid-October, and the trees were putting on their autumn glory. The day was still in shadow. At the edge of our backyard stood an ordinary shagbark hickory, a tree I had never paid much attention to. A hard frost the night before had fringed the hickory's golden leaves. I happened to be looking out the back window of our house when the rays of the morning sun first glanced off the tree's uppermost boughs. The tip of that shagbark suddenly became a golden flare, a flaming sword turning every which way, guarding who knows what gate.

Then just as suddenly, the shagbark let go its uppermost leaves and poured forth a slow, golden cascade upon the lawn. As the sun rose higher and its light fell lower on the tree, the same process—a moment of brilliance followed by a saffron rain of leaves—repeated itself, again and again, down the length of the canopy. For ten minutes or more I watched this go on, until the sun had undressed that tree entirely. I can't remember exactly what happened next—certainly some spectacular shift in consciousness would have been in order—but sights such as this are lost on suburban boys, and likely I went back to my Saturday morning cartoons. My tree remained unclaimed.

In high school I came across a quote by Saint Bernard: "What I know of the divine," he says, "I learned in the woods." This seemed like a modest improvement upon the Catholicism I was raised in. Shortly after that I read *Walden*—another improvement—and decided that I, too, would go to the woods. So in college I moved to Maine and majored in forestry, where I was taught that "trees are America's renewable resource."

Resource is one of those funny words, commonly used but understood only uncommonly. Originally it was a verb and meant "to go back to the well (i.e., the source) and get more water." Later it came to mean a substance or material recognized to have utility for society, something that can be quantified, assigned a value, and applied to a purposeful end. Usually a resource is consumed progressively as it serves its purpose, but trees, we say, because of their "renewability," escape this fate. Nowadays we speak of human resources, the renewability of which, I suppose, depends upon your faith.

In my senior year, I took a culminating course called Forest Economics. It was not designed for those who would live in the woods. In an everyday sense, the word *economics* refers to the management of the household—making the bed, buying the groceries, balancing the checkbook—but in the university economics is said to be "the study of the allocation of scarce resources." Applied to trees, this definition leads to some strange ways of talking. "In terms of production," the professor explained, "trees are unique because they are simultaneously the factory and the product. If only we could find some way to encourage them to harvest themselves, then we'd really be in business!"

Little of this style of thinking ever proved useful to me, but I still recall the slides the forestry professor showed of an old-growth redwood stand in California. The lecture hall all at once felt more like a cathedral than a mausoleum, and those photographic images might just as well have been stained glass. The redwoods towered with their greenness and handsome branches, their crowns lost in a misty rustle among the coastal clouds. Later, when I finally made it to California, I learned that the birds of heaven, here called marbled murrelets, nested in the lofty redwood boughs, and ten thousand mysteries were lodged in the fern-thickened shade of the forest floor. The professor said nothing of all this; his mind was elsewhere. "Hurry up and get out there and see these trees now," he quipped. "All those senescent stands will be harvested within the next ten years. Even-age rotations are what those timberlands need. Good forest management will take care of that."

The message was clear: in these American woods, there is no past, no poetry, only the bottom line; no ghost, no god in the tree nor angel in the air, but only the feathery schemes of experts who have the forest all figured out. When I graduated from the University of Maine in 1980, I had a B.S. in forestry, and they gave each graduate a white pine seedling, but still I had not found my tree.

Proverbs are the original field guides to life. In Russia it is said that from all old trees comes either an owl or a devil, and this wisdom holds true in North America as well. Local legends and vernacular histories abound with tales of strange goings-on connected with trees. Near High Point, New York, for instance, there is the story of

Rowland Bell, a barefoot fiddle player who lived in a log cabin and had quite a reputation as a healer. He would cut a lock of his patient's hair and place it in the hole of an aged chestnut tree that grew along the road nearby. The tree would then shake and tremble like an aspen, and the patient would be cured, the malady having been transferred to the tree. But that was a hundred years ago; chestnut blight has long since killed that tree, and today managed health care tries to keep most people out of the woods.

On the campus of a small college in the Northeast there is an ancient oak known as the "Chewing-gum Tree." Its trunk, from the base to as high as you can reach, is sheathed in a thick layer of hardened gum wads, the residuum of several decades of ruminating students who disposed of their spent quids by sticking them to the tree. The word around campus is that if you walk by this oak at midnight you can hear a faint murmuring or buzzing coming from it, said to be the voices of all those gum-chewing students from the past, still discussing long-forgotten exams or the joys and sorrows of youthful love. Some students believe that if you ask this oak a question about your future, it will tell you. Privately the administrators at the college regard the tree as an eyesore and even a health hazard (all those generations of germs!), but they fear removing it because it is supposed to have been planted by the college founder; to cut it down would be seen—at least in the eyes of alumni benefactors—as tantamount to cutting down the family tree.

The old shamans who lived in the thickly wooded Pacific Northwest had a strong spiritual connection with trees, much like the druids had with the oak in Europe. Through an assortment of rituals and charms, the shaman used his or her tree as a spiritual helper to ascend into the sky and consult with various cosmic beings in order to gain news of the other world. Among the Salish people, one of the most powerful spiritual helpers was known as "Biggest Tree," and it was claimed to aid the shaman in obtaining special gifts made from cedar. These little gifts were in fact "alive" for those who had the power to perceive and use them.

A similarly magical worldview lies at the very roots of the Great Western Tradition. In ancient Athens there was a religious sect known as the *theoretikoi*, who resorted to thick forests and quiet groves in order to conduct their meditative practices. When discussing the psyche, Aristotle often uses the term *theoria,* the root of our word *theory.* Roughly translated it means "contemplation," but it can also mean "sending ambassadors to an oracle." Perhaps this was the Greek way of seeking "Biggest Tree." After all, the most famous of their oracles was the one at Dodona, which originally consisted of an immense old oak with a spring gushing from its base. Through the rustling of its leaves and the remarkable doves that alighted in its boughs, Zeus announced his supreme will to human beings. That old oak stood and delivered its sacred messages to eager querents over many centuries, until a robber came along and cut it down. When the tree fell, the oracle fell silent forever.

Once upon a time in Japan, there was an old willow growing beside a stream. Nearby was a temple. On the other side of the stream was a village. One day the villagers felt they needed to build a bridge, so they decided the tree should be cut down and used to supply the timber. One young man among them, however, loved and respected the willow. He alone remembered that the temple had been built in the first place by their ancestors to honor that very tree. He offered other trees from his own land to the bridge builders if they would spare the willow. They agreed, and so it was saved from the axe.

Shortly after that, the young man encountered a beautiful young woman sitting under the willow. They agreed to marry, but she told him he could never ask where she was from or who her parents were. The two lived happily together for many years. The man grew very old and frail, but his wife remained young and beautiful.

Then one day the Emperor decided a new temple should be built. The village offered the willow to supply the lumber, believing that this would bring them good fortune. On the morning the tree was being felled, the man who had once saved the willow was awakened by his wife. "I am the spirit of the willow," she said. "Because you saved me once, I married you to make you happy, but now I must leave you forever. The willow is about to die, and so must I, for we are one and the same. I go now to the willow." And with that, she went away.

In America, we love our trees and keep track of the biggest in each of the species. I have visited a few of them myself. Even though none of them turned out to be my tree, they do belong to somebody. For instance, the world's largest American elm stands in Louisville, Kansas—or so it did until March 1997, when "an angry youth," according to the *Manhattan Mercury* newspaper, tossed a firebomb into a hollow of its massive trunk. Residents of Louisville, Kansas, were strongly attached to their elm and are still deeply grieved over its loss. "This random act of violence," wrote one commentator, "not only ruins a lovely, highly prized tree, it ruins a champion from a species that is seen all too rarely these days. An outbreak of Dutch elm disease in the 1960s wiped out a large portion of our nation's elms, especially in cities, where elm-lined streets became barren." There is talk about placing a memorial shelter and plaque at the site of the immolated elm. That all trees felled by human hands should receive such homage!

Earlier in this century, Aldo Leopold wrote that conservation is "a matter of what a man thinks about while chopping, or while deciding what to chop. A conservationist is one who is humbly aware that with each stroke he is writing his signature on the face of the land. Signatures of course differ, whether written with axe or pen, and this is as it should be." I suspect, however, that signatures are executed with a considerably wider variety of instruments than merely axe or pen, and for reasons far less scrutable than Leopold lets on. It would be worthwhile to talk with that "angry youth" and find out on whose behalf he was acting. Was it his tree?

The faithful in Salt Lake City found their tree in May 1997, at the corner of 300 East and 700 South. Turns out—perhaps by coincidence—that it was another elm. A couple years prior, city workers had done a little pruning on the shade trees in the neighborhood, and they removed a rather large branch from this particular tree. About a year later, a kindly old woman by the name of Graciela Garcia was walking by and noticed something unusual on the flat knothole where the branch had been lopped off—it appeared to be an image of a woman. Not only that, but a strange liquid was oozing from the woman's face. Tears!

Graciela Garcia could take a hint. She dropped to her knees and made the sign of the cross. Every day after that, she visited this tree with its dewy stigma and said her prayers. She placed flowers and devotional candles at the base of the elm, and pointed out the woman's image to curious passersby, explaining to them in her gentle way its significance. Many joined her in prayer. At night the candle-light flickered softly on the faces of the devout as they ran their fingers over the beads of their rosaries. Thus an informal neighbor-hood ritual emerged, pleasing just about everybody except the drug dealers, and it went on for several months, until somebody phoned the local television station.

A news crew was sent out. By evening, word was out: an image of Our Lady of Guadalupe had appeared, right in the heart of Salt Lake City. Not only that, the Holy Mother was weeping. To their credit, the news team made no attempt to interpret the phenomenon, yet its import was clear enough to the television audience: the image must mean *something!* An outbreak of curiosity seekers ensued, erupting around the elm like a plague of gypsy moths. At any given time, dozens of people could be seen near the old tree, many of whom were awaiting a turn to climb a ladder and stroke the image or dip a handkerchief in its liquid to be applied to faces and bodies as if it were holy water.

Although no obvious miracles occurred in connection with this particular image of the Virgin Mary, police did report a significant reduction in the number of calls coming in from this, one of the city's most crime-infested neighborhoods. It was miracle enough for some people to demand that the Catholic Church investigate the matter and declare the image an "official" religious event. Church authorities—perhaps taking their cue from recent American politics—responded evasively by issuing a terse press release: "The Catholic diocese has no knowledge of any unusual religious occurrence at a tree on 700 South and 300 East in Salt Lake City." Despite the Church's lack of commitment, the image—according to the *Salt Lake Tribune*—did bring "a sense of peace and hope to some residents of the beleaguered neighborhood."

Well, not quite everyone.

About five months after the tree was brought into the public spotlight, an obviously disturbed young man showed up one night at the tree to pray. After lighting a votive candle and placing it among the dozens of others, he disappeared into the darkness of a nearby park. A little while later his body was found hanging from a low limb of another tree, not far from the image-branded elm. An apparent suicide, he had used a length of plastic hose, asphyxiating himself by kneeling forward. "We were kind of scared," reported one witness who was a regular visitor to the elm, "because of the things he had in his hand." She was referring to the plastic hose. No suicide note was found, nor did the man have any identification. His only message consisted of two words in Spanish on his T-shirt, which the young man must have written just before killing himself. He sliced open his palm with a broken piece of glass, then wrote his last words in his own blood: *Jesus Vive,* "Jesus Lives."

It would seem that trees are as much connected with our going out of the world as they are with our coming in. For all we know, the only thing standing between eternal bliss and damnation might well be a tree.

At the center of Nordic mythology was the World Tree, called Yggdrasil. It was described as an immense ash rooted in Hell with boughs that supported Heaven. In between lay Earth. The trunk of the World Tree was an axis that linked human beings to dwellers above as well as below. There was a prophecy that, at the end of the world, Yggdrasil would provide shelter to the last man and woman, and from them would sprout a new lineage. The Old Norse word *Yggr,* which is related to the English word *ogre,* is another name for the god Odin, supreme deity and creator of the cosmos. To hang a man on the gallows was to string a sacrifice on Yggr's tree; after death he became a member of Odin's band, riding the storms with him.

To "baffle" a person once meant to subject him to public disgrace or infamy by hanging him upside down from a tree, a horrifying reversal of everything that person stood for. A public hanging, or any form of execution, is a ritual moment of suspense, requiring witness: what hangs in the balance is a question of transformation. The gallows is but one tree hung between two others. Our coffins are made of trees.

Indeed, Death traditionally has been portrayed as a forester. He was called *holz-meier,* or "wood-mower," by the sixteenth-century

German writer Geiler von Kaiserberg. In a book titled *De arbore humana,* he writes: "So is Death called the village-mower or wood-mower, and justly hath he the name, for he hath in him the proper-ties of a wood-cutter, the first of which is communitas, he being possessed in common by all such as be in the village, and being able to serve them all alike. So is the wood-cutter common to all the trees, he overlooketh no tree, but heweth them all down." Along the Columbia River, the Indians' custom was to place the bodies of the dead in boxes and sling them by cedar-bark cords from the branches of trees; eventually the cords would give way, and the bones would be strewn upon the ground like fallen leaves.

A logger in Oregon once appeared on network news. A reporter had come out to the woods to interview him at work. He took time out from his labors to answer the reporter's questions. The logger was very polite. He wore a hard hat. He resented environmentalists because they all lived in the city and said they loved the forest but knew nothing about it. "How can you love what you don't know?" For his part, the logger was intimate with the forest, having cut down a good bit of it. He did not live in the city. He knew what he loved and stood by it. Behind him stretched a vast swath of open land; stumps and slash indicated a recently removed forest.

The reporter could not resist a certain irony. She pointed to the clear-cut. "How is this love?"

Not a fair question to be asked on national television, but as that man now looked out in hopeless confusion upon the field of his endeavors, the inexplicable terrain of his love, he was desperately looking for something. Maybe his tree.

"I do love the forest," he said at last. "This doesn't look good, I know—but my family . . . I'm sorry that what we have to do is so ugly."

The words of another spiritual forester come to mind. "Too late I learned to love Thee," writes Saint Augustine in his *Confessions,* "O Thou Beauty of ancient days, yet ever new! Too late I learned to love Thee! And behold, Thou wert within and I abroad, and there I searched for Thee; deformed I, plunging amid those fair forms which Thou hadst made. Thou wert with me, but I was not with Thee." Now here's a fellow who found "Biggest Tree."

To find your own tree, a transition needs to be made. But of what kind? In psychoanalytic theory, a "transitional object" refers to something used by a child as a kind of emotional comforter. Typically it is a piece of cloth or a doll or a teddy bear. In their theory, psychoanalysts regard the transitional object as a psychological bridge that enables the child to cross from "primitive narcissism" to a more mature emotional attachment to human beings, which are the only appropriate hooks on which to hang our love, or so they say. Thus in a small child, a deep and powerful attachment to a teddy bear, or a tree, is considered normal, but in an adult such fondness for the nonhuman is a sure sign of neurosis, or worse.

Nevertheless, there seems to be something a little off about this way of describing how the innumerable relations out there compose our respective worlds. Committing yourself to the wrong theory is a major handicap to finding your tree. Pigeons alighting in the boughs at Dodona, murrelets in a redwood tree—things my forestry professors never spoke of. A lady once complained to the great American artist James McNeill Whistler that she did not see the world he painted. "No, ma'am," he replied. "But don't you wish you could?"

Earlier I mentioned that there were two trees in the Garden of Eden, and that Adam and Eve found and tasted but one of them, the Tree of Knowledge. The other tree, the tree they never attained, was in fact the biggest tree in the Garden, the one that God guarded most jealously. It was the Tree of Life. "And the Lord God said, Behold the man is become as one of us, to know good and evil: and now, lest he put forth his hand, and take also of the Tree of Life, and eat, and live forever." And so Adam and Eve were driven away, into endless generations of longing. What the Bible fails to report, but is well attested by legends surrounding the story, is that for the rest of their lives, Adam and Eve kept trying to find their way back, not for the Garden itself nor for any home they wished to reclaim, but for the Tree they never found.

After I spent most of my growing up years daydreaming of trees far north and west of New Jersey, a perverse law of compensation would have it that, as I stand on the threshold of middle age, living in the dark woods of Idaho, much of my dream life should now be spent back in the Garden State. The other night, for instance, I dreamed of that hickory tree in our old backyard. It's been twenty years since I last saw it, yet there it was again in all its flaring, turning glory. This time, instead of remaining in the house, I rushed out into the yard in order to throw my arms around its trunk and claim my tree as it shed its golden treasure of leaves upon me and the leaf-gold lawn.

But I woke up before I got there.

THE DARK SIDE OF SUCCESSION

ACROSS THE STREET FROM ONE OF THE PLACES WHERE I GREW UP WAS A big stretch of woods surrounded by a wilderness of tract houses. It was New Jersey, where woods are not as rare as you think. Improved streets there often deaden into vacant lots. In any case, the woods were thick enough to shelter stories of wild animals, buried treasure, and hoodlum teenagers.

During the twenties, somebody tried to turn the woods into a housing development. They cut down the trees and built streets and named them after trees: Elm, Chestnut, Spruce, and Larch. They put in storm drains and curbstones and even fire hydrants. The new streets appeared on the official county map. Then for some reason the houses were never built. The whole idea was abandoned, and the trees started coming back.

Over the years, it all grew up into the woods that I knew as a child. It was very strange to hike there along streets named for trees with trees growing in the middle of them and no houses, just more trees. Something very sad and lonely about that place, as if a whole neighborhood, houses and all, had gotten up and run away from home. Some called it a real estate disaster, but really it was just the trees growing back, doing what trees do. Nothing special. Forest ecologists call it "succession." It's nobody's fault.

The funny thing is, when I was a kid in the sixties all those streets named after trees were still on the official county map, even though really there were no streets in the usual sense of the word, only woods. At first I thought it was an oversight—sooner or later the county officials would have to realize this gap between their map and the territory. But year after year the streets kept showing up on the new maps, and the woods just kept getting thicker. One time for a civics class project I wrote the county officials a letter about this matter. They never responded. Nothing further followed from this, only the course of years.

I was back in New Jersey for a visit not long ago. The woods are still there, and the streets named for trees are still on the map. No accounting for it, so the gap remains. Yet, at one time I thought I could help fill that gap by studying forestry, so I went off to college in Maine and majored in it. It wasn't what I had expected.

In forestry school, where they otherwise teach you a variety of nasty tricks to pull on the natural world, they almost redeem themselves by providing students with the Story of Succession. It's one of the few things from my forestry education that stayed with me over the years. I learned it in a course called Forest Ecology, which is really just an unacknowledged kind of metaphysics for resource managers. As I was taught it, this story comes right out of the nineteenth-century book of ideas about the balance of nature. And it goes like this.

When the first European explorers showed up in New England in the sixteenth century, everything looked like a Thomas Cole painting. A century later, when the English settlers arrived at Plymouth and Boston, they looked out upon this new world and all they could see was dark and intemperate forest, teeming with all manner of savagery. The Puritans referred to their new neighborhood as a "howling wilderness," an attitude that was passed down through the generations. You can still see it in Cotton Mather, who was writing in the early eighteenth century. "Beware the Evening Wolves," he says, "the rabid and howling Wolves of the Wilderness, which would wreak Havock among you, and not leave the Bones till morning." I heard something rather like this from my forestry professors during the last quarter of the twentieth century, when they talked about those people who would save the trees.

If in addition to textbooks on silviculture and economics my fellow forestry students and I had been exposed to some literature along the lines of Butler's *Lives of the Saints* and Cotton Mather's *Wonders of the Invisible World,* our education might have had the necessary depth to understand the Story of Succession. For instance, from Butler one discovers that the name "Boston" is actually a contraction for "Botulf's Stone," which is back in Lincolnshire, England. Having gone through a forestry education, I think Botulf's Stone might actually be a better rock upon which Americans might found a myth than the one in Plymouth, Massachusetts. After all, Botulf was a popular saint in medieval times, and he seemed to practice a style of forestry much akin to our modern methods.

His calling was to march around in the still standing forests of his day, and chase out all the "develen and gostes" that made their homes there. When these poor wood sprites realized they couldn't scare away the earnest saint, they asked him why, since they had already been expelled from everywhere else, they could not simply remain in this quiet corner of the world, where they bother no one. In response, the saint made the sign of the cross, thereby forcing the poor "develen and gostes" to flee. They must have gone to North America.

Thus when it comes to Cotton Mather, you could say he was the Stephen King of his day. Long before the horror novel was invented, Mather was providing his eager readers with spine-chilling accounts of witchcraft and other varieties of demonism going on in their woods. With zeal he warned them about "Droves of Devils" that cavorted in the yet unmanaged forests of New England, ready to pounce upon all but the most vigilant of Christian soldiers. The good people of New England took heed, and hacked away at their forests until, by 1800, the wolves had been exterminated and most of the landscape had been rendered into pasture. Ah, but such victories are short-lived.

Blame it on economics, blame it on improved technology, or blame it on other wars in other places, but by the 1830s people were abandoning New England in throngs. Better land—and lots of it—awaited them in the West, so they surged forth into the setting sun. In their wake, the forest sidled back into New England, and another remarkable transformation ensued: the forest returned. The region today lies more thoroughly under shade than at any time since Cotton Mather.

The wolves took a little longer to return, but they're back now too. Perhaps you've not heard about this. That's okay. It's just a sign of how smart the wolves have become. I think it's safe to assume the "develen and gostes" are here too.

A more concise version of the Story of Succession comes from my old college notes. It takes the form of a definition, the sort we were required to memorize and repeat back on countless exams: "Succession is the progressive development of vegetation toward its highest ecological expression, the climax." As suggested by the final word in this somewhat prudish, technical description, out there under cover of the wild lurks a poem. Or at the very least a boundless passion. To forestry professors and their well-heeled students, this is worrisome.

Yet, even foresters have their renegades, the most famous of whom is Aldo Leopold (1887–1948). He went to forestry school at Yale, where he listened to an early version of the same Story of Succession I was told at the University of Maine seventy years later. If only the professors knew the corrupting influence this tale has had on certain students, I'm sure they would drop it from the curriculum.

In the case of Aldo Leopold, the story became the basis for his revolutionary Land Ethic, which he lays out in a book titled *A Sand County Almanac*. "In short," he writes, "plant succession steered the course of history." Leopold doesn't have much to say about the "climax" stage of succession, but he does go on at length about fertility ("the ability of soil to receive, store, and release energy") and health ("the capacity of the land for self-renewal"). He summed up this Land Ethic in what might be called the Golden Rule of environmentalism: "A thing is right when it tends to preserve the integrity, stability, and beauty of the biotic community. It is wrong when it tends otherwise."

By reading *A Sand County Almanac*, one quickly discerns that all this talk about nature is in fact an allegory for how one might live the good life, in the old Platonic sense of doing the right thing. This is Leopold's ecological *Republic*. Like all utopian visions, it presents an Eden or Arcadia or someplace where natural harmony prevails, much as high barometric pressure does over the West Coast in summer. Thus in terms of Utopia's weather, every day is a good day.

A Sand County Almanac was the best book I read in forestry school, but I had to discover it outside of my classes.

Of course, right from the start, the Story of Succession (not to mention any ethic derived from it) has had its critics. Among certain scientists, the Story of Succession was always already a diminished thing because, well, it's a *story*. Worse, it's less than a story—it's a *fable*. They say that those who place their faith in such narratives are willfully blind to natural phenomena, choosing not to see things as they truly are but rather as they wish to see them.

Even though the Story of Succession has been roundly rejected by these people, no one has put forth a more compelling account of the mysterious workings of the universe. Some folks just don't like stories of any kind, but they enjoy obliterating a utopia when they spot one. To all who would seek a pristine state of nature, they say: "Don't use science to prove your myth!"

I must admit, there is some substance in what they say. As the ethnobotanist Gary Nabhan puts it: "We are often left hearing the truism, 'Before the White Man came, North America was essentially a wilderness where the few Indian inhabitants lived in constant harmony with nature'—even though four to twelve million people speaking two hundred languages variously burned, pruned, hunted, hacked, cleared, irrigated, and planted in an astonishing diversity of habitats for centuries."

In early New England this idea is confirmed by Thomas Morton. He complains in 1637 that what few big trees are to be found there are located around the swamps, where the extensive broadcast fires set by the Indians each spring could not reach to do them harm. As for the rest of the region, the fires kept the woods fairly open and the trees reduced in size. Thus the forest never achieved the "climax" you hear about in the Story of Succession. "For the savages," says Morton, "by this custom of their firing the country, have spoiled all the rest, and it has continued from the beginning."

Environmental historians are fond of saying that, if ever there had been "virgin forest stable at climax" in New England, it disappeared long before the first history was ever written. Such visions of an untouched wilderness, they say, exist chiefly in the tales of other times. Thus the Story of Succession, with its ardent talk of fertility and health, with its timeworn plot that leads inevitably toward some "highest expression" of being, is consigned by more sophisticated minds to the hinterlands of myth. Yet I, for one, take comfort in knowing that there are some places not even historians can enter.

Myth is undervalued in a scientific education. To explain what I mean, I'll turn once more to my old college notes. In a wildlife-management class, we were informed about the "Edge Effect." My notes define it as "the interactions that take place in the transitional zone where one cover type ends and another begins." In other words, the Edge Effect is what goes on along the boundaries between different ecological communities or realms. The plants that grow where forest meets grassland, for instance, produce the perfect combination of habitat and food supply to encourage an abundance of wildlife. That's why the New England Indians were setting all those fires—the flames generated the subsequent growth of plants that lure elk, deer, turkeys, and numerous other animals. New England, under Indian management, was one vast game farm throughout.

Myth is a kind of edge effect. It occurs between the human community and what is *not* human. In one sense the word *myth* simply means a "telling of events," but this telling creates the proper conditions for commerce between realms. Myth is a boundary situation, placing us at the very brink of being human. It's like standing on the edge of an open grave. Look around the next time you attend a funeral. Amid all the flowers and tears, you'll see people casting furtive glances into that dark opening in the earth. Be assured, they are looking well past the bottom of the hole, hoping to catch a glimpse of the ferocious emptiness. Nowhere in my notes can I find a definition for this term.

Understanding of these darker matters must be sought in places that offer the proper cover. One such place is Henry Thoreau's journal, especially in the last years of his not-long life. Unfolding in those pages is the earliest version of the Story of Succession. So far as anybody knows, it was Thoreau who, in the 1850s, coined the term *forest succession*. But you'll look long and hard through the scientific literature before you find any mention of his name. Certainly, it was never spoken in any forestry class I took.

A critical commonplace has it that Thoreau's journal in the last decade of his life became less "literary" and more "scientific." So far as it goes, this is an adequate description. But as a diligent reader bushwhacks through the abundance of obsessive and repetitive observations that Thoreau makes about the changes going on in the eastern Massachusetts landscape—long passages that even the most generous of readers describe as little more than unusually well-written field notes—the ferocious emptiness will occasionally be seen bolting from cover. "I confess," he writes about a year and a half before his death, "that I love to be convinced of this inextinguishable vitality in Nature. I would rather that my body should be buried in a soil thus wide-awake than a mere inert and dead earth."

Another place the ferocious emptiness gives a snarl is in a story that comes from eighth-century China. The famous painter Wu Tao-tzu had just finished work on his masterpiece, a grand landscape done on a wall of the palace. It took more than a decade to complete. The only thing more far-reaching and impressive than his painting was the solitude in which the great artist pursued his work during all those years.

He kept the painting under a huge drape until it was finished. When the Emperor arrived for the unveiling, Wu Tao-tzu gave the signal and the covering dropped away to reveal an immense and awesome scene rendered in exquisite detail: there were wild mountains, pristine lakes surrounded with venerable trees, and clouds boiling off cold ridges into limitless expanses of sky. If you looked closely, you could even see numerous people at work and play throughout the spectacular landscape. The Emperor stared astonished at this fabulous country.

"Look!" the artist exclaimed, pointing. "There's a cave in the side of that mountain. Inside is a dragon. Let's go pay a visit!" He clapped his hands, and a gate suddenly flew open on the side of a mountain, revealing the entrance to the cave. Wu Tao-tzu stepped into the painting, turned around, and said to the Emperor: "Come on, it's even better inside. I can't put into words how lovely it is, I can only show you. Follow me!"

With that, he entered the cave. But before the Emperor could gather his wits and follow, the painting and the ten thousand things it contained—including the artist and the yet unseen dragon in the cave—began to fade away. In no time, everything had vanished. The Emperor was left staring at a blank wall.

The ferocious emptiness is something like that, but not so far away. You encounter it when you go back to a favorite spot of wilderness, some woodland haunt where you enjoyed a family picnic or spent your honeymoon camping—let's say it's in Idaho—only to find that the place has been "harvested" (my old college notes define this as "the removal of a crop or stand of financially or physically mature trees"). Or you return to the house you grew up in and discover the woods where you used to play are gone, and in its place are a shopping center and a lot of houses that all look alike. In this case, it's your childhood that's been harvested. Suddenly you begin to get the picture: sooner or later everything—including you—will meet the same fate. Now *that's* the ferocious emptiness.

You'll even encounter it on the tops of mountains. An acquaintance of mine recently told me about a climb he made up Borah Peak. At 12,655 feet, it's the highest mountain in Idaho. Technically, not a very difficult ascent, but according to one guidebook at least three people have died on it. Two were swept away by an avalanche, and the other lost control of his glissade and went soaring off a cliff edge, never to be seen again.

My acquaintance and his brother climbed this mountain in late summer, when the weather was clear and the snow for the most part gone. They had a safe trip, save for one unsettling moment, but it had nothing to do with physical danger.

After making the arduous hike that climbs 5,200 vertical feet in just three and a half miles, the two young men made it to the top. Out here in the West, most of the high peaks have some kind of register on their summits, places where successful climbers can sign in. It's a record of achievement, as good as pinning your name to a cloud. My acquaintance located the heavy aluminum box stashed between some boulders. He opened it to take out the notebook that holds the names, but was surprised to find the box filled with dirt. "It was the weirdest dirt I've ever seen on a mountain," he told me. "I wondered how it could have gotten into the box. I figured it must be the wind.

"So I reach in there and feel around till I come up with the notebook and pull it out. It's filthy, covered with all this gray dust, and so are my hands and clothes at this point. It's even getting in my mouth. There's no water up there so I have to live with it for a while. Anyways, I shake the book off and hand it to my brother. He opens it to the page with the last entry on it so we can sign in. He starts reading for a moment and then screams, 'Oh, shit!' and throws the notebook down on the ground. 'Oh shit!' he keeps screaming, 'Oh shit!'

"'Kerry, man,' I say to him, 'what's wrong? What's the matter?' And he looks over to me and says, 'That's not dirt. The last entry in the notebook says it's some guy who died a couple weeks ago and they cremated him. That's his ashes! His son must have come up here and put them into the register. What the hell was he thinking? Oh shit, and you've got him all over you!' "

I like then to picture these two young men, bounding their way down the mountain, one of them screaming "Oh shit!" and the other spitting as the dust unfurls behind him like a banner, until far below, among the sheltering trees, they find a clear stream where they might wash away this memento mori obtained at higher elevation, and thereby purge their memory of this man they never knew, and forget their sudden encounter with the ferocious emptiness.

Perhaps by now you see where this—and the Story of Succession—has been leading.

Among the pantheon of ancient Greek deities, the only one who had no altar dedicated to him was Hades, lord of the underworld. That's because he is everywhere and requires no special place or temple to make his appearance. Your mortal body is altar enough. He just shows up, unbidden. In many ways, he is the most generous of all the gods, bestowing his blessings wherever he roams, and that's why he acquired the nickname Pluto, which means "wealth" or "riches." Everybody loves him. Or should. In fact, the running joke in ancient times was that whoever pays him a visit is so overwhelmed with his beneficence, they just can't bear to leave. If this wasn't so, far more people would return from his kingdom than has been the case.

"Nature loves to hide," says Heraclitus, who wrote a whole book on the subject and then hid it away in a temple. What fragments we have from this fugitive text suggest that Nature is yet another nickname for the lord of the underworld. Wisdom too may be found in the treasure house of the charitable Hades, which is why philosophy can be defined as "the practice of death."

And so we come full circle to the Story of Succession, the dark side of which is death. As in forests, so in the seral stages of life. Even speech has its Story of Succession, as pointed out long ago by Augustine, in an Aldo Leopold kind of way: "Not everything grows old, but everything dies. . . . That is the way our speech is constructed by sounds which are significant. What we say would not be complete if one word did not cease to exist when it has sounded its appointed part, so that it can be succeeded by another." Meaning itself, we must conclude, is yet another of those gifts that come up from below.

Today when you ask college students what their goals in life are, they commonly respond "Success!" The transient ground upon which they chase their dreams constantly gives way to yet further ground, similar in kind. "Success is counted sweetest / By those who ne'er succeed" is Emily Dickinson's version of this same story.

The dark side of succession, the ferocious emptiness, reveals itself in the clear air of a high granite peak, in the ultraviolet fragrance of a flower that grows only there. Or it stands forth in the green shimmer of a mountain meadow, in the icy flicker and blinding flash of a waterfall in winter, or in the quiet amazement of fields and forests all across New England as the moonlight pours down upon sleepers in warm beds. Or it's there in the autumn, when the leaves let go one more time in the roaring cascade of years.

You see it too along the thousands of golden-arched "Miracle Miles" all across America, leading back to that very first dream of success, where everything becomes transparent as hunger pains in the very belly of being. And you see it in New England where the forest first came back in the old burial grounds, places barely remembered and hardly noticed anymore, where shade was expected and even welcomed. As trees crowded in among the graves, the letters inscribed on the markers simply let go from the cold stones, and fluttered down to the ground like leaves. In this way word followed voice back into the quiet earth.

OUT OF BOUNDS

THERE ARE SEVERAL VERSIONS OF THIS STORY, BUT THE POINT OF EACH IS
the same: a colossal error was made. The Idaho we have is not the
Idaho we should. The people who live here are haunted by images of
a bigger, better place, a birthright that has somehow been denied, by
someone we know not whom, for reasons never made clear. Large as
it may appear on a map, Idaho, as we know it, does not suffice.

The year is 1864. The United States Congress for its own reasons
decides that, as far as the West is concerned, the Idaho Territory isn't
enough—or perhaps it's too much—so the place is split in two. A
survey party is dispatched to run a boundary along the crest of the
Continental Divide, the line of Rocky Mountain summits that separates the watercourses flowing toward the Pacific from those flowing
toward the Gulf of Mexico and Canada's Hudson Bay. Nobody back
in Idaho knows what's going on.

The surveyors set out on their mission. Sometimes the forest is so
thick they can barely read their instruments. Other times they find
themselves on high, barren mountaintops, exposed to the elements
and huffing for thin air. There are long stretches of snowfield where
they sink up to their waists, and the reflected sun renders their
exposed skin into jerky. It's hard and miserable work, but these
surveyors do what they must. They stick to the plan and proceed in
meticulous fashion along what they believe to be the divide, hewing

to their prescribed route no matter what cliff or bramble or bear's den presents itself as an obstacle. That is, until they encounter a river that cuts right across the range and their way. Woops!

A mistake has been made. By definition a continental divide suffers no breach of flowing water. The bemused surveyors look at the troublesome river, then at each other, then back at the river. Their reputations are on the line. For many months they have been blazing their way northward, planting their stakes and raising their boundary monuments—*along the wrong crest*. It's way too late to redeem this work. Let it be remembered that they are men of science. How will they recover from such faulty discrimination?

One of them scratches his head. Another shrugs his shoulders. Then somebody mutters, "Who'll ever know?"

Without another word, they aim their transits due north, ignore any further flukes in the terrain such as mountain range and watershed boundary, and dash off the remainder of the distance to Canada as a straight line. (Take a look at your map, see their handiwork for yourself, and praise it as it proves.) Then the surveyors hotfoot it out of there back to Boise to collect their money before anybody is the wiser and figures out that Idaho has, in fact, suffered a huge territorial loss: Missoula, Butte, and a vast chunk of forsaken paradise all lying within the greater Columbia watershed. "It should have been ours!" says the Idahoan. Then, to add insult to injury, those who today live on the other side of the bogus boundary—now called Montana—have the audacity to refer to their state as "The Last Best Place."

There is another story—this one told by historians—that says the tale I just told you is apocryphal. They say the truth lies elsewhere. Their version would have it that in 1864 when Congress passed the statute that split Idaho and established the Montana Territory, the boundary was fixed clearly and definitely right where it is now. Not only was there was no faulty survey, but there was *no survey at all*. At least not at that time. It was not until 1904 when an actual boundary survey between Idaho and Montana was conducted, but by then the legend of the faulty survey had already sprung up. Myth, the historians tell us, had already blazed its own boundary long before the flesh-and-blood surveyors got around to fixing theirs.

Nevertheless, most Idahoans ignore the historians. That tale just doesn't provide any emotional satisfaction. You could say that the people of Idaho live with an overarching and inexpressible sense of loss, so they remain attached to the faulty survey story as a kind of origin myth. It does not matter that its plot line extends from a commonplace blunder, for it gives the citizens a sense of coherence on a grand scale.

There's a long tradition of boundary lore out there. Generally speaking, boundary lines that are defined by natural features—ridges, rivers, and seashores—don't require monuments to indicate their location, but those determined by lines first conceived in the imagination and then projected upon the terrain must be perpetuated by marking. With satellite imagery and geographic information systems, all of this may be changing, but in the old days it was important for a surveyor to get out on the ground.

An old surveying manual on my bookshelf says: "We can not impress on the surveyor too strongly the necessity of planting, at each corner established by him, permanent monuments for future reference, from which subsequent surveys may be made. . . . This will permit future surveyors to find the original corners more easily and thus enable them to do at least a more satisfactory job. The more accurate the work, the less liable to end in litigation." In his *Laws*, Plato proposes a harsh punishment—namely, the wrath of Zeus—for anybody who messes with boundary lines: "Sooner let a man try to move the largest rock that does not mark a boundary, than a small stone separating friend's land from foe's, and established by an oath sworn to the gods." There may be something to this.

Once when I was backpacking in the southern Sierra, a wilderness ranger told me about a guy who was suspected of stealing old U.S. Geological Survey bench marks from the tops of mountains. One day this man's charred body was found on the summit of Bronto Peak. His hands were gripped around the patined bench mark that was still secured to the rock. It looked as though he was trying to dislodge it when tragedy struck out of the blue. The ranger attributed it to lightning.

꘠

A little to the south of Boise, Idaho, out on the arid plateau above the Snake River Canyon, is a singular low butte that rises from the sagebrush plain like some oversized Hershey Kiss. It is called Initial Point. An odd name, but this is the odd place where Idaho began, at least in a certain sense, because the first official land survey of the state was initiated here. In surveyor jargon, an "initial point" is a designated landmark from which true lines are extended north-south and east-west to establish township and section boundaries. It's a clever and elegant way to bind wildlands to human ideas of order. Why this particular place should have been selected as the initial point for mapping Idaho is immediately apparent when you go there: from its modest summit you can see all of creation, or at least that portion of it we say is southwestern Idaho.

I've only visited the spot once, right after I moved to the state, and it was by accident. I was looking for someplace else, but I wound up here. As I was driving down a road in the middle of a treeless nowhere, I could see the butte rising solitary from the otherwise unwrinkled plain. It called attention to itself. It had a little elevation, so it seemed to insist upon its individuality. Then I saw the sign, "Initial Point." There was an arrow pointing toward the butte, so I turned off the paved road and drove a mile down a dusty washboard till it ended in a small, round valley below the summit. Where the road stopped was another sign. It said the tiny valley was the caldera of an old volcano.

I parked the car, grabbed my binoculars, and climbed to the top of the butte. It wasn't difficult and there was another sign, a brass plaque mounted in stone. The plaque was riddled with bullet holes. Still, it praised the deeds of some government officials, and, using the logic of a writer who never expects to be held accountable for his words, suggested that Initial Point is the Plymouth Rock of Idaho.

Later I found out most of these signs were installed by the Bureau of Land Management as part their "interpretive program." They want to make sure a visitor receives a proper history of the place. Historians and surveyors are really a lot alike—dead serious about their respective disciplines. Nobody writes a "funny" history, and nobody wants a "funny" survey. Like property rights, the past is fleeting: if you don't get it into a book or onto a sign, it gets away and goes feral.

Done with the signs, I turned to enjoy the view. That's when I noticed a big white pickup truck barreling down the washboard road

toward the butte. Out here in the Wild West, big pickup trucks
roaring up to meet you are cause for anxiety, even when they don't
have a gun rack mounted in the rear window. But this one did—I
could see that with my binoculars when it came to a stop right next
to my old Corolla. A middle-aged cowboy got out of the twenty-four-
valve turbo diesel Dodge Ram, along with his rifle.

As if this was not distressing enough, the back of the truck was
jammed with lawn ornaments. A dozen or so of them. There was a
bird bath and a "gazing globe," as well as a colorful assortment of
plaster statues, including a bashful girl, a frog under an umbrella, a
couple of curled sleeping fawns, an elf riding a pig, several Garden
Angels, a plump cherub sitting on a toadstool, and the Virgin Mary
with her arms outspread in a gesture of beneficence. Given that there
were no lawns out here in the desert, I found this cargo troubling.

The cowboy leaned his rifle against the truck. He lowered the
tailgate and went to work. One by one, he removed the lawn ornaments, taking each into his arms and walking it over to a nearby slope
of cinders, where he carefully arranged them into a line. When the
last one was in place, he returned to the big white truck, picked up
his rifle, and took aim. Then the shooting began.

The gazing globe went first, bursting in a vicious sparkle. Next, the
elf got it, blasted right off the back of the pig. Then the Virgin Mary
went down, but not without resistance—she required several rounds.
Nevertheless, chunk by chunk—first ear, then chin, then nose—she
was at last reduced to rubble. The cowboy then turned his weapon
upon the remaining victims and let loose, squeezing off shot after
shot—CRACK CRACK CRACK. It was a lawn ornament massacre. He had
to reload a number of times before the job was done. Sometimes a
bullet missed, lodging instead in the dark earth, where it raised a
small cloud of dust that took to the air like a ghost.

By this point I was hustling down from the summit. Since all the
action was happening next to my car, little chance I could get out of
there unnoticed. The etiquette of the great outdoors requires you to
make polite small talk with strangers encountered along the way. I was
obligated to say something to this cowboy like "Howdy! Fine day,
isn't it?" or "How's that old Ram running, anyhow?" or maybe
"Yeah, I hate Garden Angels too. Can I have a shot?"

He saw me coming and got in the first word. "This must look pretty strange," he said. He was wearing Redwing work boots. In the dust next to his left foot was a cherub's head. He kicked it out of the way so we could talk more directly. "I'm going to tell you why I had to do this."

"You bet," I said. There was nowhere to go.

❧

His name was Anatello. Funny name for a cowboy, but it turned out he was originally from Gloucester, Massachusetts. When he was a small child, say five or six years old, he used to play down by the fishing docks. One day, some older boys thought they'd have a little fun with a stinky old fishing net they had found near the wharf. They got the idea it would be entertaining to throw the net over some unsuspecting victim, preferably a helpless one. Anatello was their catch. Having snared him in their net and hauled him in among some garbage cans behind the packing plant, they left him to extricate himself, all alone.

He was terrified, bound so tight he was unable to move arms or legs. He could breathe okay, but the stink coming off that old fishing net made him sick to his stomach. He rolled and thrashed and screamed for help, but nobody came. Utterly without hope, all he could do was cry from the depths of his being.

"I wasn't worried that I was gonna die—that would've been an escape. I was scared shitless I was gonna be stuck in that horrible net forever, that I'd never be able to move again. There's no running from terror like that. You can't get away from yourself. And the whole time I'm smelling that awful fish."

Eventually he was rescued, but not before the course of his life was changed utterly. As soon as he came of age, Anatello moved away from Gloucester to the wide-open skies of Nebraska for a few years, then on to settle in Idaho, where he could dress like a cowboy and have nothing to do with the ocean. "I don't ever want to see it again," he says.

Anatello's horrifying encounter with the fishing net is long in the past, and he has had a good life since. He's been married for twenty years and is happy living on a ten-acre ranchette outside of Nampa.

56

He works for the Idaho Department of Transportation, where he helps to maintain the network of state highways. His job as a thoroughfare survey engineer (TSE) requires him to drive around the state in a van with a video camera mounted on the dashboard, recording the condition of the roads. He does not drive very fast. Sometimes he stops to take a look under a bridge. Work like this is performed all the time in large agencies in order to cover liability. The state does all it can to avoid litigation. With thousands of miles of highway in Idaho, it takes Anatello three years—with weekends off and three weeks' paid vacation per annum—to cover all the territory. Then he starts over again. So far he's gone through seven complete cycles and is working on his eighth. Rather than in years, Anatello has come to measure the span of his life in the survey rounds he makes of Idaho's roadways.

Last week, while he was away on the job, Anatello's wife attended an estate sale held in an old barn near Weiser. A great aficionado of arts and crafts, she was immediately taken by a collection of lawn ornaments she saw crowded into a back corner of the barn. None of this "yard art" was antique or even special, but she was drawn to it nevertheless and was able to purchase the whole lot for twenty bucks.

The lawn ornaments were loaded into the back of the big white truck, and she drove them home and set them up out in the front yard: the bird bath and the gazing globe, the bashful girl and the frog under the umbrella, the curled sleeping fawns, the elf riding the pig, the Garden Angels, the cherub sitting on the toadstool, and the Virgin Mary in all her beneficence. Because the Anatellos lived far from any neighbors, nobody complained about the effect this crowd of kitsch might have on property values. Nobody complained, that is, until Anatello got home that weekend.

As soon as he pulled up in the van and saw all those lawn ornaments, he knew he had arrived at big trouble. His stomach felt sick in exactly the way it did the time he was caught in that stinky fishing net more than forty years ago. He had attended Catholic school while growing up in Gloucester, so he knew that statues—even lawn art—are not *just* statues but lures for disembodied spirits. When it comes to receptacles of any kind, it is well said: sooner installed, sooner come. Perhaps only a psychologist can fathom why Anatello made the link between the stinky fishing net and these lawn ornaments now in his yard, but his gut had always told him that nothing is truly very far from anything else, and that weird things especially are never remote from one another. He wasn't going to wait for this Virgin Mary to wink at him or wave or—Lord help him—start walking around the yard. He was going to take prompt action.

After making his way gingerly through the demonic minefield of his yard, Anatello burst into his house and remained only long enough to tell his wife that he was loading up those lawn ornaments and taking them someplace they'd never do anybody any harm. Anatello's wife was dumbfounded. She begged for an explanation but never received one; some things just cannot be spoken of. Anatello, for reasons of his own, had never told his wife about the terror he had endured in the stinky fishing net, or how once in a while he still has a nightmare about it. It was his emotional Achilles' heel, the kind of thing a man can tell only to a stranger met in a bar or on a trail. Even then some extraordinary compulsion—such as an angry god or a guilty con-science or maybe just emotional exhaustion—is necessary to get him to unload.

The last glimpse Anatello's wife had of her lawn ornaments was something like this: the sun flashing off the gazing globe as the big white truck barreled down the driveway. Perhaps the sleeping fawns had been jostled from their slumbers. And the Virgin Mary may have been rocking, back and forth on her plaster feet.

❧

When he finished his tale, Anatello made it clear he had nothing more to say. I was free to go. As I pulled out in my old Corolla, I got one last look at Anatello. He was reloading his rifle. The image was framed in my rearview mirror as it is now in my memory. I never saw him again.

Driving away from Initial Point, I made my way back to the Snake River. Before long, I came upon an unusual local landmark, a toll-booth-size block of basalt covered with ancient and still undeciphered petroglyphs. Locals call it "Map Rock." All the doodling on it is said to compose a map of the Snake River and its tributaries, chipped out by some ancient cartographer as if to guide travelers through unfamiliar territory.

Historians, of course, have a different story about this rock: they say there is no story. Or at least none to which we are privy. The petroglyphs may look like a map to us, we who are the products of a culture that uses cartography as an instrument of power and knowledge, but to those prehistoric people who inscribed this rock the figures could only have meant something quite different. I don't know how these historians can be so sure they are right, but for once I prefer their story, since it tumbles that boulder back out of bounds. The world once again becomes a place where anything might happen, where even lawn ornaments get a chance to play.

A few days later, while browsing around the library, I came upon an old U.S. Geological Survey Bulletin that contains a photo of four men identified as the 1908 Idaho-Washington Boundary Resurvey party. Each man looks like a scraggly-bearded Henry David Thoreau as he appeared in the last years of his life. These men of the 1908 Idaho-Washington Resurvey party have taken time out from relocating the boundary markers set by their predecessors in order to pose for the photographer and posterity. The men are standing on the trunk of a tree they have felled. On either side of them is the dense forest. Behind them is the signature of their work: stretching as far as the eye permits, a fifty-foot-wide gash through the dark and brooding woods. Under the photo a caption reads: "Vista Cut Along Boundary Line." The photo was taken right *on* the line, but there's no way to determine which side might be Idaho, which Washington—it all looks the same. Only the gap in the forest suggests a difference. No telling what cold eyes may be peering from the somber gloom.

For some reason, Anatello came to mind as I was looking over this picture. I got to thinking that, perhaps in his world, the vista cut along the boundary between reality and imagination, between what is reasonable and what is ridiculous, was too narrow for his own good. But then, what about the rest of us in the so-called ordinary world? Might our own vista cuts be too *wide*? When it comes to the human psyche, how reliable are the surveys upon which we stake our claims to truth? In any case, the boundaries seem to have been established in various ways for reasons perhaps never to be fathomed. Yet, ancient wisdom makes one thing quite clear: mess with a boundary, and you'll pay at the hands of the gods. Not that this has ever stopped the reckless.

Initializing Idaho, initializing a life. The witness trees are blazed, the vista cuts are made. Given enough time, nature itself will see to it that the boundaries become obscured, the blazes on the trees over-grown, and the monuments toppled over in the dark reexpression of the woods. Then at last, the extravagant life might once again be pursued and the marvelous tale allowed to unfold—all of it out of bounds.

Until the next survey is extended.

TRANSLATING THE WORLD

I ONCE KNEW MAN WHO BECAME TAKEN WITH AN ORACLE. UP UNTIL THAT point, he had been a promising young scholar of literature, writing a thesis on the poetry of John Milton, but somewhere along the way his reading took a peculiar turn, from *Paradise Lost* to tarot cards, from literature to divination. He became mad for meaning.

At first, the tarot was just a curious game; he didn't believe the cards held any special power. But he quickly discovered they "worked." A spread of cards—the Magician here, the Two of Swords there, the Fool upside down on top of it all—constellated for him a significance as potent as the heavens do for astrologers. He found the cards could predict the future—or at least *his* future—and they were particularly expressive in matters of the heart. Women had always refused to go out with him, but now he had welcome counsel. It was all in the cards. He expanded the range of his divinations to include the outcomes of hockey games, horse races, and the stock market, though the metes and bounds of his profit were strictly psychological.

He consulted the tarot for help in writing his master's thesis; the cards became a kind of ghostwriter. He submitted draft after draft of this curious collaboration to his professors, only to have them send it back for revision, again and again. They criticized a certain evasive quality in his argument. Still he persevered for seven years in this project, until the tarot told him to abandon it. By this time he was laying out the cards each morning before he got out of bed. If the reading was unfavorable, he stayed at home that day. It was a habit that cost him a series of jobs and all of his friends, but the cards vouched it was for the best.

Then one day he just gave up the tarot altogether. It was believed the cards had a hand in this. Shortly afterward, he walked into my office, scrutinized me from the ashtrays of his eyes, and handed the deck over to me. "This is a gift," he said, "but there's one condition."

There's always a condition.

"Never," he intoned from the grim privacy of his heart, "do a reading for yourself. Only read for somebody else. Otherwise you'll end up like me." He walked out of the office, and I never saw him again.

The path this young man took is perhaps more compulsive than most, but his yearning for order and significance in life betokens both an alienated majesty and some familiar behavior. Each of us, in various ways, is on a quest for meaning. We call it our life's journey. The trail is blazed with omens: the sparkle in our beloved's eyes, the storm on our wedding day, the letter from an old friend far away. There is no shortage of signs, and though most are left unread we say this is a good thing.

Poetry and prophecy stream from the same source, which Plato called "divine madness." Whether we plumb the depths of creativity through a great poem or a deck of cards, we are engaged in divination. The red sky in morning gives sailors warning, and the spin of a bottle leads to a first kiss—all hints pointing toward where the treasure of our buried lives may be found. Divination is consultation with the gods: "Let's see how they feel about our plans." Their response serves as a moral barometer of human action within the greater context of the universe, and divine influence often extends further than everyday words can express. The language of poets and prophets may be as close as we can get, because—as the old saying goes— "After word comes weird."

This reflects an intimacy on a cosmic scale. "Earthly things must be known to be loved," Pascal remarks, and "divine things must be loved to be known." We are constantly divining the joys and sorrows of those we love. "What's up?" we say to each other in greeting, as if to indicate there's more to our relationship than just the two of us. Love goes by contraries: whether a friend, a lover, or a god, one's relationship with the other is always both ordinary and extraordinary, exhilarating and fraught with perils. One courageous woman I know refers to her practice of astrology as "making out with the gods." She is otherwise unattached. Whatever your own beliefs, it's a safe bet to behave as if the gods *are* there and they *do* care what we do.

The word *oracle* refers to the divine message itself, the actual response of a god to a particular question, but it also refers to the vehicle of communication; thus, a spiritual "medium" is a human oracle. Anytime the ego is thoroughly suppressed, the personality lies open to mediumship. Beware! Cavorting with gods is hazardous—you become a psychological lightning rod. Sleep, alcohol, narcotics, and hypnosis are familiar methods of inducing this state, but an agitated emotional condition works just as well. We still speak of "demonic possession," though academic psychologists are doing their best to veil it in terms such as *dissociative personality disorder.* And most of us have experienced a nightmare, but few are aware that the word is derived from Old English and means "night incubus" or "goblin."

Some years back I bought a deck of tarot cards at a bookstore in Portland, Maine. The young woman at the register, after noticing my purchase, told me about a "Mystery Cruise" she had been aboard out in Casco Bay: "A woman there was reading tarot cards for people, but I didn't go to her. I don't want to know my future." A long pause ensued, and then: "Is that a bad thing?" Ignorance in this case may indeed be bliss because, unburdened by foreknowledge, we proceed through our days more blithely. To know the future with certainty would be to empty Pandora's box even of hope. If there is an order to the universe, as most seem to believe, and if that order can be discerned as scientists say, or divined as poets and prophets say, to what use will that knowledge be put? In oracles begin responsibilities.

Divination is a family of languages not truly taught in our culture. An aspirant must nevertheless be schooled in the symbolic nuances of a vast corpus of signs or omens, such as the lines on the palm of a hand, the flight of birds across a field, or the configuration of planets in the night sky. To acquire these languages demands as much effort as any other tongue. Some who attempt them will fail; others will go on to achieve various levels of fluency; but only a few ever become true poets.

In a famous passage from Plato's *Ion*, Socrates goes on at length to say how all great poets "have their excellence, not from art, but are inspired, possessed." The god, we are told, "has bereft them of their senses, and uses them as ministers, along with soothsayers and godly seers . . . in order that we listeners may know that it is not they who utter these precious revelations . . . but that it is the god himself who speaks." Plato draws a sharp distinction between the medium—the "true diviner"—and the interpreter who, resorting to the gift of reason, is composing a story, a translation of the prophet's experience. Do not mistake the text for the prophecy, he warns. Likewise, the poem is not the words on the page but your *experience* of the words, of the world they open up for you.

Poets, astrologers, tarot card readers, and other seers into human character—including social workers, psychotherapists, and pastors— must be able to apply their narrative gifts in a convincing and responsible fashion. In other words, they have to be able to tell a good story. The future is *always* a story. For an audience to commit themselves to a narrative, they must be taken in by it; to resist is to refuse an invitation, which sometimes is the wisest course. When it comes to a particular future—whether that of an individual or a nation—the "true" story is the compelling story, the one you believe, the one you live by. The choice is yours.

It's easy to go astray in these interpretive realms, just like the young man with his tarot cards. He sacrificed too much; instead of being a coauthor of events, he became a pitiable minor character in the story of his own life. The Greeks in Plato's day had an adage: "Only those who have their wits about them can judge about themselves and their own affairs." When it comes to oracles and poetic consciousness, possession is 100 percent of the law: either you possess the power or it possesses you.

Consider this story from ancient times. A group of friends procured what might best be described as the ancient equivalent of a Ouija board. They had a few questions. The device consisted of a tripod made of olive wood, the apex of which supported a metal dish.

Engraved around the rim of the dish were the twenty-four letters of the Greek alphabet. The procedure was very simple. One of them held a ring suspended on a fine linen thread above the plate, while the rest of them stood around and made long-winded invocations to some vague deity of prophecy. At last, they got the thing to work.

The ring began to swing from letter to letter, spelling out words that eventually gave appropriate answers to the various queries the group made. Then one of these wise guys popped the question they had all been eager to ask: "Who shall be the next Emperor after Valens?" Ever so slowly the ring on the thread began to spell out the answer: "*theta* . . . *epsilon* . . . *omicron* . . ." Seeing "Theo" spelled out in this way delighted the group. They had their answer. "Ah-ha!" they exclaimed. "The next Emperor will be Theodorus." They broke up the session and went home.

Later that evening, one of them made an indiscreet boast to the wrong person. Shortly afterward, the whole prognosticating crew was arrested and brought up on charges of treason. They were swiftly tried, found guilty, and executed. Just for good measure, Theodorus—who had no part in the group and knew nothing about their activities—was also put to death.

Had the oracle been wrong? Not at all. Seven years later, Valens himself was killed. He was succeeded by a man named . . . Theodosius.

Like any translator from one language to another, oracles are notorious for their unreliability. Sometimes the gods just don't have any message. Other times, all we get from them are enigmatic sayings and cryptic images. "The lord whose oracle is in Delphi neither declares nor conceals, but gives a sign," says the dark Heraclitus. Nevertheless, when you are dealing with any interpretation, the capriciousness of gods is a minor problem compared to the errors of human judgment. Tragedy is the outcrop of our *mis*-taking the signs. Because the oracle speaks a symbolic language ("gives a sign"), the literalist treads on treacherously unstable ground. The oracle is a form of allegory, which in classical rhetoric means "speaking otherwise than one seems to speak." It may be the word of a god, but the god speaks figuratively.

Make no mistake: dabbling in oracles is very dangerous business. Had those men standing around the tripod been a little less hasty to interpret, they might have avoided the particular fate they fell into.

The wise person in these interpretive matters must be like the wily Odysseus, ready, not to suffer fate, but to participate in the making of destiny. "For some things," as Seneca explains, "have been left so in suspense by the immortal gods that they turn to our advantage if prayers are directed to the gods, and if vows are undertaken." Upon this point the whole question of fate versus free will turns.

Across the street from me when I was growing up was a family who conducted weekly charismatic prayer meetings at their house. Rumors flew around the neighborhood about the weird goings-on over there, everything from levitation to out-of-body travel. At one point I started going to these meetings because there was this girl . . . Anyway, they would sing songs and play guitars and offer up little prayers to Jesus. For the most part, pretty ordinary stuff. But then there came a moment when things decidedly shifted to another level.

There was a boy in the family named Tommy. At the time, he was about thirteen years old. All the songs and prayers and hugging one another were just a warm-up to the part Tommy played in these gatherings, because suddenly he would "go all angel-eyed" and start bellowing in deep guttural tones, giving tongue to ghosts, gods, or I don't know what all. The sounds he made flowed and held together like a language, but there was something about it that seemed profoundly "made up"—though not by Tommy. Linguists refer to this uncanny form of speech as glossolalia. Tommy's family called it "speaking in tongues"; they said it was the voice of the Holy Spirit. I for one could feel a presence in that room but was skeptical about its identity. Spirit? Yes. Holy? I wasn't too sure.

Tommy, or "the Holy Spirit," would speak his unplumbed speech, uninterrupted, for ten minutes or more. I remember wondering: is this how they talk in heaven? I had more questions; they remain with me. Do you have to learn this language before God lets you in? Do the dead speak to each other? And what do they have to talk about? I remember how lofty and moving Tommy's not unlovely monologues were to hear. I never understood a single word of these discourses, but they were always affective: they left me feeling sad. What was he saying? Who was *really* doing the talking? And didn't this spirit have anybody else for company, save for this room full of mixed-age and unremarkable suburbanites? The dead must be very lonely.

In his first letter to the Corinthians, Saint Paul writes: "One of them receives the gift of tongues, another that of interpreting the tongues." When Tommy-the-Holy-Spirit concluded his inscrutable discourse, the father—a stern man whose few joys included wielding absolute authority over his family—would interpret what his son had just said: pleasantries about God's love for all his children. Yet, something, I am sure, was forever being lost in translation. The father's pedestrian words in his everyday New Jersey accent were never so compelling as the dramatic, unfathomable, and oh-so-lonesome utterances of the son.

It is said that a genuine experience of divine possession is traumatic and has the effect of shortening the medium's life. Tommy's experience was genuine. If only some of us there had been more skillful in our abilities to interpret his oracular pronouncements, we might have descried where all this was leading. In later years, Tommy began to hear voices. At first, there was only one, which he took to be his guardian angel, but this voice was soon joined by another, then another, and another—until these companions in spirit became a mob, and a riot broke out at the very center of his soul. At last, Tommy leaped from an interstate overpass, plummeting to his end in a mundane snarl of rush-hour traffic.

Although the interpretive difficulties with oracles are usually not so manifestly tragic, they are always anxiety producing to those who, by temperament or experience, are not accustomed to this style of consciousness. As a teacher of literature, I have found that when college students encounter deep symbolism for the first time—in the works of such poets as William Blake or Emily Dickinson—their initial response is usually befuddlement. Attempting then to press forward in their interpretive endeavors, they next experience irritation, which quickly leads to frustration and finally open hostility. In the face of the demands these works make upon them, they are stripped of their cognitive maps. They are deep in the woods and have lost the trail and are beginning to worry about bears.

"Why can't they just say what they mean?" is the lament of these young people who are making the first tentative steps into the vast and dubious terrain of poetic consciousness. "That's life," I tell them, speaking literally. How often do human beings "just say what they mean?"

The true, the poetic reading is the one in which the work and the audience become one. Confounding and risky as all forms of poetic consciousness are, they compel us to step into the same meaningful space from which the oracle itself was drawn. Augurs in ancient Rome called it the *templum*. That has a nice ring to it, but I also like the poet Charles Olson's term for it: he just calls it SPACE. "I spell it large because it comes large here. Large, and without mercy." Pop psychology is fond of saying that each of us has a need to create a "personal space." Imagine the shock then, suddenly to realize, right in the pit of your stomach, that "Space reaches out from us and translates the world," as Rilke expresses it in one of his poems. To enter this space you must be alert to pattern; you must believe that it is okay to talk about human experience and nature in terms of repetition and broad generalization. Good fences might make good neighbors in the literal realm, but here among poems, prophecies, and dreams, the boundaries may well be clouds.

The dangers of poetic consciousness are outweighed only by the rewards, which have nothing to do with absolute pronouncements on meaning and on what will or will not pass, but instead consist of revelations that the future is not fixed but boundless, and that what gods there may be are eager for our participation. The choice is ours. "Things here are signs," says Plotinus. "They reveal therefore to the wiser teachers how the supreme god is known. The informed student reading the sign may then enter the sacred place and make real the vision of the inaccessible." Those who return from these darkling territories bring with them messages. Those messages are poetry. Let the interpretation begin.

THE SHADOWS OF DOUBT

"WE ALL HAVE OUR GHOSTS," A FRIEND OF MINE IS FOND OF SAYING. Perhaps he is more haunted than the rest of us, for he believes that ghosts are behind all human passion, animating those moments when an otherwise composed individual suddenly loses it. You fall in love, and that's a ghost having its way with you. Rage? Just another ghost. Courage? Cowardice? Crankiness? All ghosts. Any behavior for which you are at a loss to explain yourself, when you shrug your shoulders and say, "I don't know what came over me"—*that*, my friend will tell you, is the work of ghosts.

Skeptics dismiss any talk about ghosts and hauntings as the product of a disturbed mind, and there is some truth in this. I have to admit, even though I have had my own experience with ghosts, I sometimes worry about my friend. A pall of melancholy hangs over him, some relentless inversion in the weather of his soul. He talks about his ghosts not only at parties but also around the office, so he struggles to keep an everyday job. His real work lies elsewhere. By avocation he's a poet, but very few people know this; even fewer have read any of his verses. Perhaps when it comes to artists, a disturbed mind is a creative mind, a sensibility not content with the way things are. My friend may have a hard time holding down a job, but he is never at a loss for words, or company; after all, there is commerce between him and the ghosts.

Wasn't it Socrates who said that poets are "not in their senses," that they are possessed by a *daimôn*? Socrates, who was not known to hold a regular job, frequently consulted with his *daimôn*. He was as much a poet as he was a philosopher. The Greek word *daimôn* is usually translated as "guardian spirit" or "divine power," sometimes "demon," but "ghost" serves equally well for people like my friend and maybe even Socrates. These people *are* possessed. No wonder Plato's imaginary Republic was not open to poets: they are the primordial troublemakers, the great unsettlers.

A ghost is popularly believed to be the disembodied spirit or soul of a dead person. It shuns the light and lurks in dimly lit places, so we call it a "shade." In Homer's *Odyssey,* the dead in Hades are depicted as "flittering shadows," and in the *Metamorphoses,* Ovid renders them as "bloodless umbrage wandering without body or bone." Dante's hell is packed with shades, and the dead hover as "empty images" for Aeneas on his visit to the underworld. The most poignant expression of this phantom reality is found in the *Iliad,* when the bereaved Achilles encounters the ghost of Patroclus. Achilles reaches out to embrace his beloved friend, but the ghost just dissolves into the ground with a thin cry. "Oh my!" laments the grief-stricken Achilles. "Even in the House of Hades something is left, a soul and an image, but no flesh and blood." Just to assure you that more than a literary convention is at work here, consider that among California Indians, ghosts were said to take the form of human beings, but were ashen in color and shadowy in substance. And only recently, near where I live, there were reports of a young boy who complained to his mother about the "whispery people" who wouldn't let him sleep at night. "What do you mean?" the concerned mother asked. "The shadows on the ceiling keep talking," the boy explained. "They sound like flies. They want me to come with them." The family quickly moved out of that house, but I fear we may have lost a budding poet.

Usually a ghost is shy, preferring to make appearance to one person at a time, or to a small, intimate group, often children or teenagers. Mostly, the living stand in passive relation to ghosts: the wraith happens *to* you, even though you might be minding your own business, as when, say, you're peeling potatoes one evening by yourself in the kitchen, or you're walking up the poorly lit stairway that leads to the apartment of your new lover. It comes unbidden, like a dream. Dreams, in fact, are the most likely place to encounter ghosts. Most of us have met them there, even if we can't remember.

Every once in a while, there is a bold one among the living who takes a more active stance toward the "other side" and seeks to invoke a ghost or two. For sometime now, seances and Ouija boards have been the divinatory methods of choice, especially among the young and the reckless, but such practices are not without risk. There is so little control, so little between ourselves and all hell breaking loose. Without discipline, ghosts will run amok. The problem for the spirit conjurer is identical to that of the poet: how to unite freedom with precision. Overheard in a coffee shop the other day, one young woman severely admonishing another about the dangers of amateur seances: "Just one wrong move, and Poof! Suddenly every dead rock star and TV evangelist is knocking at your door and forcing you to bake ten thousand apple pies. You can't trust these ghosts. They have a mind of their own." Another way of expressing it: start invoking them, and ghosts become like birds at a backyard feeder—once you put it out, you get endless flocks of regular visitors demanding to be fed. You better be prepared.

The psychologist Gustav Fechner, that great nineteenth-century precursor of William James and Sigmund Freud, offered some very commonsensical advice: "The simplest way to guard oneself against the coming of ghosts is not to believe in their coming; for to believe that they come is to meet them halfway." Poets, of course, are the great believers, and they are impetuous to boot; not only do they meet the ghosts halfway, but they will also go to extraordinary lengths to pay them visits in their dark home. Think of Orpheus singing his way into the frightening softness of the underworld to retrieve his beloved Eurydice, or Dante jostling through the hopeless shades to the very center of Hell. Not easy journeys.

The Buddha warned his disciples not to waste time speculating about the afterlife; that will take care of itself. Better to focus on your life here and now, and live it to the best of your abilities. From this perspective, ghosts are important not for what they tell us about our destiny on the other side, but for what they bring to light in this very moment. They may come just to roust us from our sleep. Ghosts carry with them treasure from the unfathomable depths. Hades, the god who rules this shadowy realm, was also known as Pluto, which—as you recall—means "wealth" or "riches." Another of his epithets was "the nourishing one." So you could say that to hear stories of ghosts provides some kind of psychological nourishment. Likewise, to tell such stories, again and again, is equally nourishing. There is no gap between great literature and everyday experience. The ghost story is a venerable genre, from Homer right down to last night's campfire when, as the embers were burning low, somebody was heard to say, "Let's have a ghost story."

Let me tell you what happened to me once. It was very strange and occurred several years ago, when I was still living in Maine. I had graduated from college and was thoroughly lost as to what I should do with my life. I was depressed. One day I'm driving on this back road down toward Mount Desert Island to visit my friend Westphal. There are no houses along this road, only thick woods. At one point, I drive past a clear-cut strewn with innumerable pale granite boulders, probably dropped there by the last glacier. They are shining in the late-afternoon light, and I think of tombstones. No sooner does this thought cross my mind when suddenly all these people stand up, one from behind each rock. How strange! What are they doing out here in the middle of nowhere? Then something even more strange happens. They all start rising up, floating into the air. They aren't so much people as they are vaporish figures in the shape of people. I can see their faces. They're laughing. They begin to run in the same direction I'm driving. They lope across the clear-cut and into the standing woods. They float, they leap in long strides, they laugh the whole while. I'm terrified, but all I can think is, why are they laughing? And why are they following me? I grip the wheel and stare straight ahead at the road. Out of the corner of my eye I can see they're keeping pace with me. Around the bend, an old cemetery comes into view. It really is a cemetery—there's a wrought-iron fence around it. These running, laughing ghosts, or whatever they are, stop and gather in the cemetery, but I keep going. I turn my head for one last look, just in time to see them still laughing, sinking now into the ground, one behind each tombstone. The last figure, clearly a young woman and smiling, looks at me and waves.

I've thought about this doubtful episode repeatedly over the years. I remember at the time thinking: is this really happening? I remember the long wisps of their bodies streaming like smoke as they ran. I remember the impish look on the face of that ghost-woman just before she dropped out of sight. I remember the goose bumps. And I remember how depressed I was. Sometimes I wonder: Did I make this whole thing up? Was I just going nuts? Then I tell the story again.

Lately I've been having doubts, so the other night I phoned back to Maine to talk to Westphal. Surely, I must have said something to him at the time about the ghosts who cavorted alongside my car on that strange afternoon so many years ago. Surely, he would remember; surely, he could corroborate. I recounted the story to him. I asked: "Do you remember this?" There was a pause. "O'Grady," he says at last, "that sounds like some story I'd tell my kids."

Life is full of doubts, and nothing is more doubtful than ghosts. Nevertheless, in those uncanny moments, when the firm ground of your belief is suddenly jolted, when you have by an experience that shakes you right to the core, a door flies open and a mysterious figure stands there bidding you come in. Your choice: accept the invitation, walk forth, and perhaps go mad in the process; or you can turn tail, hurry away, and hope you can get back to that solid old familiarity, if it's still there.

In ancient China there was a renowned artist, an old Taoist who painted nothing but ghosts. One day, when asked why he never painted anything else, such as a horse or a dog, he replied: "Everybody knows what those things look like. If I painted a horse or a dog, there would be no end to criticism then. Ah, but ghosts! Nobody knows what those look like. I paint ghosts and everybody says I'm a genius!" *Genius*, by the way, is another word used to translate *daimôn*.

The other evening, I overheard somebody say to my poet friend: "Tell us again about the ghosts, how they make us do the things we do in love." What ghosts lurk in the dim recesses, bearing what gifts or terrors or both, will vary from person to person, and from age to age. Along the tenebrous fringe of our quick minds, the Muses themselves may be fluttering, or the dark Eurydice cowering, or the patient Virgil waiting to conduct the next errant poet on a hike into hell. Or perhaps the darkness is only thickened by the maundering shadows of dead rock stars and TV evangelists demanding our continued attention. Yet, even they, I am sure, are enough to reanimate a world that has been stripped of soul.

My friend is right: we do all have our ghosts, for a ghost is none other than that mysterious urge that leads each of us down to the dark wells of creativity. Today, under the aegis of a no-nonsense rationalism, few encounter this urge in the form of ghosts. Only children and the truly possessed see these figures beckoning from the shadows. Yet, somehow or another, in the wake of god or guardian angel, muse or lover, all creative individuals can still find their way to the source. The ghosts are there, invisible. Invoke them, and they will appear.

LOOKING FOR THE DUTCHMAN'S TREASURE

EVERY TREASURE HUNT BEGINS WITH A GOOD STORY.

Back in the thirties there were a lot of gangsters in New York who had a lot of loot to hide. The city wasn't safe, so they resorted with their booty to the Catskill Mountains and stashed it where wolves and Natty Bumppo once roamed. Have you ever seen these mountains? They are shape-shifters, or so it seems as you're driving north from the city. Every glance in their direction reveals some change in their hue and form: one moment blue, the next indigo; first they are a ripple of hills, and now an escarpment lofting like thunderheads on a summer day. Secrets abound in these mountains, and they are wondrously well preserved: every treasure ever buried here remains safely hidden, even to this day.

One night in the early spring of 1933, a big Packard pulled off on a lonely road somewhere deep in the mountains, in a forest far away from any house. Two men wearing gabardine trench coats and fedoras got out of the car. Outfits like this usually mean gangsters, and in this case it was Dutch Schultz and his henchman. Dark pines towered above them. An owl may have been watching. Nearby a stream roared with the memory of winter. The air was chill. By the light of a lantern, each man's breath could be seen hovering like a ghost till it rose up and hung itself on the branch of a tree.

Dutch Schultz and his henchman opened the trunk of the Packard and took out a pick and a shovel. They began to dig in the gravelly soil and grubbed out a serious hole. From the back of the car they hefted out a shiny steel chest, three feet long and two feet wide and eighteen inches high. Inside were millions of dollars in greenbacks, gold coins, diamonds, and negotiable bonds, or so the story goes. With great effort, the men hauled their burden to the edge of the hole and lowered it into the depths. It made a jangling thud when it landed. The Dutchman took one last look at his treasure before they closed it into the earth. The shiny steel of the chest sparkled with the light of the lantern, or was it the stars?

The Dutchman made careful work of this operation because, like anybody who hides a treasure, he had legitimate security concerns. Although his profession required he be skilled in cracking wise, when it came to the important stuff he could keep his mouth shut. Other mobsters around the city suspected the Dutchman had buried a vast horde, but they had no idea where, so they waited for him to slip up. He never did.

In the end, the steel chest remained in the ground. For reasons having little to do with treasure, Dutch Schultz and his henchman were gunned down by fellow mobsters one night in a Newark chop-house. The Dutchman himself survived the shooting and hung on in the hospital for several hours. On his deathbed, he gabbled in a fever-induced delirium, each word a polished semiprecious gem of non-sense: "Oh, Mama, Mama, Mama . . . I'm a pretty good pretzler . . . sir, get the doll a roofing . . . I am sore and I am going up and I am going to give you honey if I can. . . ."

The cops, who were interested in the treasure, sat by the Dutch-man's bedside and listened to his gibberish and asked him questions, but they couldn't get a straight answer. The mortally wounded gangster kept calling out for his mother. A psychologist in attendance said that this meant the Dutchman had returned to the helplessness of childhood and was crying out for comfort and protection. The cops nodded in agreement; they were used to deathbed scenes.

At one point, the Dutchman said: "The sidewalk was in trouble and the bears were in trouble and I broke it up." That caught the cops' attention. It was a baffling thing for anybody to say, but especially a dying gangster who had a treasure on his mind. Everybody agreed, this was no time to be literal. So they listened for more talk about bears, but Dutch Schultz fell into unconsciousness and that was it. From the treasure hunter's point of view, his last words were never adequately interpreted.

The henchman, on the other hand, was a more imprudent character. A secret usually outweighs the treasure it conceals, and talking about it is a way of disburdening. Before he was killed in the chophouse massacre, the henchman unloaded, mentioning to a few friends his part in burying the treasure—always a mistake. Pretty soon the story was out: everybody in the underworld had heard a version of it. Next thing you know, bands of hoodlums in gabardine trench coats and fedoras were prowling the Catskill forests and digging a lot of holes. They didn't turn up much except worms. Then a rumor got out that the henchman had drawn a map and given it to a friend, so this friend was relieved of both the map and his life. Now with directions in hand, the mobsters were giddy with a sense of imminent success. Treasure hunters live for such moments.

The map was said to have consisted of a crude drawing of some pine trees, a creek, and a strange figure that some argued was the eye of an owl and others the footprint of a bear. The formidable obstacles to success were now evident: the map used a code nobody could crack, the only men who had actually seen the treasure were both dead, and none of these mobsters from the city had the woods lore to conduct a proper search for a drink of water much less a hidden treasure. Besides, they were mobsters and had other business, so they gave up the search. The treasure, as far as we know, is still in the ground. As for the map, like the library at Alexandria, it was lost.

But a story like this has a life of its own. It fell into the hands of ordinary people, where it has been passed like a baton across the generations. The legend of Dutch Schultz's treasure inspired a wide range of people, from little kids listening to the story around the fire at summer camp, to high school students looking for something to do on a Saturday night, to men past their prime rehearsing fictions down at Pandora's Tavern. On a good weekend, the parked cars of treasure hunters line the back roads of the Catskills. Take a walk in the forest at this time and you will hear the soft, arrhythmic clinking of picks and shovels as it floats between the trees, a light mist of unearthly percussion, as if a band of sprites were working some fairy mine always just out of sight.

If you've ever met treasure hunters you know they are not easily discouraged. They are irrationalists, enthusiasts, the last of the great idealists. There is something wistful and intense about them; you can see it in the eyes, which reveal a wealth of emotion but seem to focus on some distant and cloud-hidden prospect. Seized by longing, they are undaunted by those who insist that the treasure is just a myth. When everybody else thinks they've gotten to the bottom of things and come up empty-handed, along comes the treasure hunter with a divining rod and he begins to dig.

Proverbial wisdom, however, warns that to have a treasure is a fear, and not to have it a grief. There is a man in Maine who gave up everything to pursue treasure. He grew up on a stretch of the coast frequented by pirates in the eighteenth century. A lot of treasure was supposed to be buried around there, and this man has spent most of his life looking for it. You could say he is a performance artist of sorts, reading the landscape as others would Homer and Virgil, Dante and Milton; he thinks the great poems of heaven and hell have already been composed, but the great poem of the earth has yet to be brought forth.

I knew him in college. He was one of those high-strung people you see on campus who is constantly snacking on nervous energy and washing it down with a Coke. The back of his car was filled with all the junk that goes with being a treasure hunter: picks and shovels, a metal detector, tattered maps to places nobody cared about anymore, and an old book called *The Gaining of Treasure and the Wonders of Hill-Digging,* the most remarkable feature of which was its advocacy of the use of forest fire as an effective method to "clear out the rank obscurities of pernicious vegetation."

He was always rushing off on some new expedition, prowling the back roads of eastern Maine for pirate treasure. Whenever he came upon a likely spot—which he always judged by its "feel"—he would pull over and commence sweeping the area with his metal detector. He wasn't like other treasure hunters, who content themselves with recovering rusty old buttons, watch fobs, and Indian-head pennies—

he would go only for the "big one." I asked him once what he knew about Dutch Schultz's treasure, and he took it as an insult. He was one of those seekers who made it a point of pride that his quest was for "real treasure" and not some mere loot. As far as I know, this man has never come home with any treasure, but his want of success is offset by sufficiency of faith.

Eventually, the man married and had a couple of kids. By all accounts, he had a happy family life and was making a good salary as a land surveyor, but he was never able to overcome his real passion. His greatest fear was that somebody else would get to the treasure first. He noted that over the course of history, the great religious figures pretty much offer the same advice for those who would seek treasure: "Go light." He took them at their word. He abandoned his family, quit his job, and now spends most of his time on the road, where he sleeps in his car. He lives a mean and solitary life digging holes on other people's property.

Where there is wealth to hide, fear keeps the best guard. In ancient Rome the state treasury was housed in a vault underneath the Temple of Saturn. They knew what they were doing. Saturn was the god who ruled over how people paid for things; he was the great cosmic accountant, keeping a cold eye on all manner of debits and credits. Those under his restrictive influence were said to be dark, melancholy, and withdrawn. Some might say stingy. The old astrologers called him the "Greater Infortune." He hung out in places most people avoid, taking delight, according to one Renaissance occultist, "in Deserts, Woods, obscure Vallies, Caves, Dens, Holes, Mountaines, or where men have been buried." Saturn's name in Greek was *Kronos,* "Time." Even today, that old god still commands a fearsome respect when he picks up his scythe and does a little gardening; we call him the Grim Reaper. Since time is money, who better to guard over a treasure?

Another group that falls under the influence of Saturn is philosophers. The study of philosophy is a kind of intellectual treasure hunt. Although I've never been very good at it myself (professors in college told me my attitude was too "literary" or "not serious enough"), I've always enjoyed bushwhacking around in metaphysical thickets. Not long ago on campus I saw a sign advertising a lecture by a young philosopher titled "A Sound Argument Concerning the Existence of

God." Seemed like directions to a treasure to me, or at the very least a chance to witness the academic equivalent of a guy jumping Hell's Canyon on a motorcycle, so I hastened to the lecture hall.

The young philosopher talked about possible worlds and actual worlds, conceivable truths and necessary truths, reflexivity, symmetry, and transitivity. The talk was intended to be taken literally. In very precise terms, he explained why his premise—that God exists—is true. Among other things, he distinguished "an invalid inference form and its suspicious conditional brethren" from "a valid inference form and its unfailingly trustworthy conditional brethren." It was sort of like the Hatfields and McCoys of the head.

Keen as I am for any method that would allow me to distinguish between the suspicious and the trustworthy, I was unable to follow the argument, which is to say I lost the trail. There could well be a treasure in the logical woods, but at a certain point I realized just how unprepared I was to find my way around out there. I became a lot more interested in just getting home safely. It may have been when the young philosopher said, "I will now proceed to disambiguate my terms." That's when I fled for the door.

Not long afterward, I was driving down the highway during rush hour and saw a billboard with a generous black-and-white photograph of the Dalai Lama, who was wearing his robe and smiling down upon the passing motorists, some of whom were flipping each other off. In the upper-right corner of the billboard was a small, almost inconspicuous, rainbow-colored trademark of a computer company. Above it was a laconic piece of advice: "Think different." In matters of great abundance, brevity is always desirable.

Nowadays there is much talk about the way things are in Tibet, but persecution there is nothing new. At the beginning of the ninth century, all the Buddhists were either killed or driven out of Tibet by a king named Lang Darma. Before they left town, however, the Buddhists stashed many of their books and sacred objects under rocks and in caves and in other wild places to prevent their destruction. These holy items, to be revealed when the time was ripe, were intended to breathe new life into the practice of future generations of Buddhists.

Over the succeeding centuries, many of these texts and objects did come to light; the Tibetans called them *termas,* a word that means "treasure," and those who found them were called *tertöns,* "treasure discoverers." A *terma,* in fact, can be understood as anything that is precious or worthy of preservation. In addition to books and relics, a *terma* can manifest as a tree, a rock, a bear, or even a special place, perhaps one untrammeled by human beings. The forms such treasure may take are innumerable, and each age finds the specific *termas* appropriate to its spiritual needs. Imagine that some of those earnest Tibetan Buddhists from long ago managed to find their way to North America and conceal some of their *termas* here, perhaps in the Catskill Mountains. Or in Silicon Valley. Or maybe where you live. Who knows but that this computer I'm writing on is not a *terma?*

One summer when I was a kid, my brothers and I were out looking for Dutch Schultz's treasure in a stretch of woods that, by our reckoning, had to be the one depicted by the symbols on the henchman's long-lost map. There was a creek, and there were some pine trees, and we had heard there was a bear around here some-where, or maybe an owl. This was the place, no doubt. Certainty such as this is one of the treasures of childhood, along with the ability to abandon yourself to a necessary imprecision.

The banks of the creek were thick with daisies, and the air was fragrant with wild mountain thyme. We dug around for a while but had no luck, so decided to give fishing a try. We had some line and a hook but no bait. We went digging for worms. It was a dry summer, and we didn't find any. Then one of us had an idea: why not try fishing with a flower? It was a big joke, so we baited the hook with a daisy and dangled it into a deep pool.

Almost at once, a fish fell for it. There was a tug on the line, and we lifted a huge rainbow from the creek. To judge from my brothers' faces you would have thought a pot of gold had been raised. We hauled it in, and it smelled like a waterfall. We didn't know what to do with it because even when we had gone fishing with real bait we had never actually caught anything before, and besides, nobody in our family liked fish anyway. So our catch lay flapping in the summer sun on the summer grass. It seemed like a shipwreck turned inside out.

I don't know what came over us—we were boys not usually disposed to compassion—but without a word we worked together to unhook the fish and return it to the creek. It darted back into the depths. Afterward when we told the story, a lot of people expressed dismay, not that we had caught a trout with a daisy, but that we had released it back into the water. "You should have held on to it," they said. "What good is a fish if you don't eat it?"

Perhaps they had a point, but today what I remember, more than the taste of any fish, is the look in my brothers' eyes when we pulled that rainbow out of the creek—the pure joy of knowing that one of the great things in life had just happened.

D. B. COOPER, WHERE ARE YOU NOW?

D. B. Cooper, where are you now?
We're looking for you high and low.
With your pleasant smile
And your dropout style,
D. B. Cooper, where did you go?
　　　　　—"D. B. Cooper, Where Are You?" (folk song)

IN THE PACIFIC STANDARD MIDAFTERNOON OF NOVEMBER 24, 1971, NORTH-west Airlines Flight 305 was about to embark in rain from Portland, Oregon, to Seattle, Washington, the last leg of a long and prosaic milk run begun that morning in the nation's capital. Outside, this close to the ground, the weather was a factor. Taking the middle seat in the last row on the right side of the plane was a "nondescript middle-aged man" in a business suit. He carried a briefcase, and he gave his name as "Dan Cooper," afterward misidentified by the press as "D. B. Cooper." Testimony perhaps to his overall slipperiness, even his alias was elusive.

After settling in like any other passenger, he placed his briefcase on the unoccupied aisle seat beside him. Soon after takeoff he handed the flight attendant—in those days called "stewardess"—a folded piece of high-quality bond paper. Unceremoniously, she stuffed it into her pocket. "I thought he was trying to hustle me," she would later report. He shook his head, gestured her to read. He moved his briefcase to the unoccupied window seat beside him. Digging deep into her pocket past sudden dread, she retrieved the note, unfolded it, and read: "Miss—I have a bomb here, and I would like you to sit by me."

She sat by this nondescript middle-aged man in a business suit. She looked at him. He was wearing dark glasses. He had a briefcase. She looked out the window, saw sky above the clouds; up here, the weather was not a factor. The man opened his briefcase on the unoccupied window seat beside him. The stewardess was shown his next bomb: a large battery connected by a maze of copper wire to eight long cylinders of what looked like dynamite. He closed the briefcase. He spoke: "Would you please return that note to me?" His voice was gentle; he was polite.

She handed the note back to him. Her hand was trembling. He slipped the note into the inside pocket of his suit jacket. It was a fine weave of wool. What now? Soft as clouds, he said: "Take dictation, a note for the pilot." What choice but to turn scribe, embrace complicity? She had to provide her own paper, but she was about to become a coauthor. Words flowed from his mouth. Words flowed through her hand. Shaky penmanship would suggest an uneasy collaboration:

> I want $200,000 by 5:00 p.m. In cash, in twenty-dollar bills. I want two back parachutes and two front parachutes. Make them sport parachutes. When we land, I want a fuel truck ready to refuel. No funny stuff, or I'll do the job.

She had no interest in funny stuff. She did her job, delivered the note to the pilot. When she returned to her seat, the nondescript middle-aged man said thank you. This note in the stewardess's hand would prove the only surviving text of D. B. Cooper.

What followed in the gathering gloom of that grim and chill November evening was circling, three hours of it, over Sea-Tac Airport, the time it took for Northwest Airlines to come up with the two hundred thousand dollars—in stacks of twenties—but not time enough for the FBI to come up with an effective response to this man wearing a suit. All agreed: this was a novelty in the annals of skyjacking.

Law enforcement was at a loss. They had been drawn beyond the pale. Nobody had a map. Here they were without protocol. Before this, no hijacker had ever asked for a parachute. Before this, no hijacker had ever demonstrated such precision, such cordiality, such grace in executing his escape. Before this, no hijacker had ever commandeered a plane for so pure a motive as D. B. Cooper's. He was not commonplace. He was not violent, rude, or slovenly. He had no complex political motives. He simply wanted the money. Bold, bright, and clean, this was the clarity of greed! Something everyone could understand.

Among the workaday, here was a technique to be envied, even publicly admired. Which is why this man became a folk hero. In later years, a Portland librarian was known to confess: "I've thought about ways to get a lot of money like he did, but I would never really do it, so I'm glad for him." Not uncommon either was the sentiment of a betweeded professor of literature who said, for the record: "Anyone who has the guts to parachute out of a jet in the middle of a dark and stormy night has my admiration. I hope he got away with the money and I hope he's not dead."

Apparently, none or few of the passengers aboard Flight 305 on that dark and stormy night knew what was going on. The pilot informed them that the plane had developed mechanical problems, that they were circling "in order to burn up excess fuel before landing"— ordinarily most disconcerting news, but apparently not to these fated passengers, who were remarkably content in their circling, in their calm burning of "excess fuel" in the unsettled night sky over Seattle, Washington. It seems that even without complimentary drinks, they were set at ease by their captain's voice; something in its imminent authority they found soothing. Everything was under control. They could sit back and enjoy their circling. Reported one of the passengers later: "He could make you feel good even if you were walking toward a guillotine."

At last the plane came back to earth, touched down at Sea-Tac in early evening and steady rain. The money and parachutes were delivered; the thirty-five passengers and two of the three stewardesses were released. D. B. Cooper could not afford release of the pilot and copilot: somebody had to fly the plane. Nor could he afford release of the stewardess: somebody had to be the hostage. When his inspection of the chutes revealed standard military issue, D. B. Cooper became noticeably peeved. He had ordered sport parachutes, the sort that enabled extended free falls from high in the sky. These workhorse military chutes would not do. With an artist's rancor, he sent them back, along with the name of a skydiving shop where the proper type of chute could be obtained. All of this delayed things. Beyond the tarmac, however, officials who did not necessarily like each other nodded gravely. In retrospect, all agreed that, except for the parachutes, the events were well scripted.

While everybody waited for the proper chutes to arrive, the nondescript middle-aged man in a business suit kept his middle seat in the last row on the right side of the plane. His briefcase remained on the unoccupied window seat beside him. He instructed the remaining stewardess to sit in the aisle seat beside him. The money was in a heavy canvas bag stenciled with the words SEATTLE FIRST NATIONAL; it rested nearby in the aisle itself. D. B. Cooper had taken off his dark glasses; his eyes were said to be blue. The stewardess looked out the window, now dark; she could see drops of rain streaking down on the outside of the glass. D. B. Cooper moved his hand to the inside pocket of his suit jacket, removed another folded piece of high-quality bond paper, gave it to the stewardess. In his soft-cloud voice he said, "Please take this forward to the flight crew, have them read it, then return it to me."

She cooperated, delivering the dispatch to its intended audience. It was a typed note with no mistakes. It directed the crew to fly the plane to Mexico City. "Fine," the pilot said in his authoritative voice, "but tell that guy this plane can't go that far in one jump—we'll need to make two interim fuel stops." The pilot had no typewriter—his was an oral transmission. The stewardess hastened back with the pilot's message. D. B. Cooper listened politely to her news. She then returned the typed note. "Fine," said the unruffled man, now folding the used note with care, now returning it to the inside pocket of his suit jacket, now withdrawing another folded piece of paper. This time it wasn't high-quality bond. "Please deliver this to the pilot," he said.

It was a standard-issue government form, typed and meticulously filled out: a Federal Aviation flight plan. "Then return it to me," he added.

When this latest curiosity reached the forward cabin, the flight crew puzzled over its precision. *Follow flight path Victor 23 south, toward Reno, Nevada.* Quizzical looks were exchanged. D. B. Cooper's route purposely avoided the wild, wooly wags of the Cascade Mountains; temperatures there would be well below freezing, snow would be falling. In the lowlands would be rain. What kind of hijacker was this, both experienced in the diving of sky and possessed of extraordinary skills in navigation?

At one point, a rain-lashed official in a trench coat walked up to the door of the plane. He was from the Federal Aviation Administration and was very wet from the weather. He requested permission to board, apparently an attempt to reason with the skyjacker. The hard things are glorious. Permission refused. D. B. Cooper now suggested to the pilot, via another specimen of that now disturbing high-quality bond paper: "Let's get this show on the road. Return this note to me." It was a moving communication. The proper chutes suddenly arrived. The note was returned. The show once again took to the air.

Onward to Reno. Not long into the dark sky, D. B. Cooper's hand returned to the inside pocket of his suit jacket. The stewardess shuddered. D. B. Cooper presented her with an appendix to the well-composed flight plan. This one read: "Maintain an altitude of 10,000 feet, lower the flaps to fifteen degrees, hold the airspeed to 170 knots. Return this note to me." The stewardess took it to the flight cabin. More quizzical looks. The pilot frowned. These operating conditions were just about the minimum for keeping a 727 aloft—and at 10,000 feet in this part of the country there were mountains out there to worry about. But D. B. Cooper knew what he was doing. The flight path he had chosen kept them over the lowlands, over the open fields scored by Interstate 5.

Bewilderment now moved aft with the stewardess. She returned this last note to D. B. Cooper; he folded it and slid it into the inside pocket of his suit jacket. Then he reasonably requested her to help him open the exit door leading to the aft cabin stairwell. No typed letter, no high-quality bond paper. They were past all written words. Now it was strict performance, direct action. D. B. Cooper picked up his briefcase from the unoccupied window seat beside him. He had the stewardess lead the short walk to the aft of the cabin. The 727 is the only commercial jetliner that has a door beneath the tail. Ordinarily, it is not a good idea to open it in flight. But given the drastically reduced speed and altitude, a reasonably safe parachute jump might be made. Besides, this man claimed to have a bomb, spoke words that seemed like clouds with mountains hiding in them. Even without typed instructions on high-quality bond paper, the stewardess complied. She showed him how to open the door. Then he ushered her forward to the cockpit and locked her in with the flight crew. That was the last anybody saw of D. B. Cooper.

A little after eight o'clock, perhaps somewhere over Lake Merwin on the dammed Lewis River in southwestern Washington, a light flashed on the instrument panel in the cockpit of Northwest Flight 305, indicating that the rear exit door had indeed been opened. Dropped the cabin pressure to that of the summit of Mount Hood. Dropped the temperature to seven below. Dropped too, it would seem, D. B. Cooper, suited for business, with two parachutes, a briefcase, and a heavy green burden. Unseen into the wild dark.

Of the three or five military jets bird-dogging the truant 727, none sighted any chute openings. The weather was inclement; sullen clouds continued to roll in from the Pacific; at 10,000 feet there was no visibility. When, on the far side of California's Sierra Nevada, Flight 305 punched through the clouds and landed at the Reno airport, D. B. Cooper was nowhere to be found. He must have jumped. A four-state manhunt was launched. APBs were flashed from Nevada to Washington, nearly the entire length of the Cascade Range. But efforts were concentrated in 150 square miles of thickly resistant forest near the Washington towns of Longview and Ariel, just north of Portland. Here, authorities reckoned, was where he jumped. Here, authorities discovered, the forest was uncooperatively dense, the terrain amply crenulated, sufficient not only to hinder an effective search but also to present a serious hazard to the cavalier sky jumper who descended into this thicket bereft of visibility, bereft of warmth. D. B. Cooper, on the threshold of his leap, was not known to have had ample protection from the elements. A business suit, a briefcase, a heavy canvas bag: anything could have happened. Said one member of the posse after a week of unsuccessful searching: "We're either looking for a parachute or a hole in the ground."

Three decades have passed. No parachute, no hole. But ballads have been composed, films have been made, books have been written, impostors have come forward. The pilot and the copilot of Northwest Flight 305 have since retired. The stewardess long ago quit her job and became a nun. D. B. Cooper is still being sought.

His remains the only unsolved skyjacking in U.S. history. The weather may have been a factor.

"IS THIS THE ROAD TO THE EDWARD JAMES?"

THE EDWARD JAMES WAS A FANCY RESTAURANT OUT IN THE MIDDLE OF nowhere, famous for its steaks. The building, by all accounts, was an old farmhouse that had been renovated, expanded, and made chichi. This happened after the fields around it had been let go. Years passed. Thick forest and everything that goes with it closed in, rendering it a rather obscure location for a fancy restaurant. But that didn't stop the people in expensive cars from coming.

Frank Sinatra sang there once. He had come for the steak, but the proprietor talked him into performing, right there on the spot. The guests were thrilled. Another time, Patty Page showed up. She didn't perform, but word has it she enjoyed watching the bears. That was the other thing the Edward James was famous for. It had a refuse heap at the edge of the forest, and the bears would come in from the wild to enjoy it. With a drink in your hand, you could watch them from the porch, frolicking in the trash, and it was well known that if you waved to these bears, they would lift a paw in return salute. There were lots of stories like this about the Edward James.

To get there you had to travel an unpaved road lined on either side with immense wolf maples. It was a desolate route by urban standards, with no streetlights, no other houses, just the Edward James at road's end. Beyond that, only an inhospitable mountain. People with expensive cars usually avoid roads like this for fear of getting lost or breaking down or worse. You can never be too careful. All roads that lead to the middle of nowhere arrive at the same place, but there's no telling where one of these lonesome highways might begin. You could be on one right now and not even know it.

The road we lived on must have looked a lot like the one the Edward James was on. In those days, it wasn't paved and it had a strip of grass running down its middle. Along the way was an abandoned burial ground—you had to know when to look—but mostly the road coursed through lonely and shagged Catskill forest as it headed up Paradise Hill. Since ours was the only house on this road, whenever people were lost—and this happened three or four times a week—they'd turn in our drive and pull up nearly to the door. They never got out of the car to come knock—they'd just sit there, expecting you to come to them. When you did go out to see what they wanted, a car window would roll down and somebody inside would bark: "Is this the road to the Edward James?"

No, you tell them politely.

"Well, where is it?"

Sorry, you say, but you don't know.

"Haven't you heard of the Edward James?"

Yes, you've heard of it. You've heard quite a bit about it.

"You've heard of it but you've never been there?"

That's right.

"So you have no idea where it is?"

It must be around here somewhere, you admit, since so many people come by asking about it. But never having been there yourself, you are loath to speculate. You wouldn't want to mislead anybody.

"Well, what about this road? Where does it go?"

Dead end, you say.

"So, this isn't the road to the Edward James?"

No way, you insist, shaking your head.

That usually ended it. The window would roll up, and the expensive car would head off. You could tell those people were really irritated with you for not knowing where the Edward James was, or maybe they were irritated with the Edward James itself for not being easier to find. No telling. But when they got to the end of the drive, the people in the expensive cars always turned the wrong way, *up* the road toward Paradise Hill, instead of back the way they had come, despite what you told them about the dead end. It's as if people like this need to see such things for themselves—they never take anybody's word for it. Ten or fifteen minutes later, usually, you'd see them pass by again, this time maybe on the right track because they never turned in a second time.

At some point, the Edward James burned down. For a while, it was big news on the Mountaintop. Even bigger news was the realization that not a single person from around here had ever been to the Edward James. In fact, *nobody* knew where it was. But the biggest news of all among locals was the realization that, for all these years, the whole Mountaintop had been suffering the same problem: strangers in expensive cars pulling up and demanding directions to the Edward James. Who were those people? And did they ever find what they were looking for?

Well, wherever they came from, word must have traveled slowly, because for years after the Edward James burned down, the people kept coming. At least once a week an expensive car would pull up, its window would roll down, and a stranger inside would bark: "Is this the road to the Edward James?"

Nobody had the courage to say that the Edward James had burned down. Decency requires that even rude strangers be given directions. So we would just tell them: "No, this isn't it. But the road you want looks a lot like this one. You're not far away now."

BODEGA HEAD

THEY CALLED IT THE "GLORY HOLE." SEVENTY-THREE FEET DEEP, 142 FEET in diameter. It took two expensive years of excavation to open the hole, the work being completed in October 1963. Spoils from the site had been used to construct an access road across the tidal mudflats at the northern end of the bay. Along the scarified shoreline of Campbell Cove, heavy equipment stood poised, ready to begin the next phase of construction. Final federal approval, expected at any moment, was all that remained between this and the earnest work.

The place, about sixty miles north of San Francisco, is called Bodega Head, but on a map it looks more like a thumb. Connected to the mainland by a wide, undulating east-west trending series of sand dunes, Bodega Head is a rocky spit of land, two miles long by half a mile wide, jutting southward into the Pacific Ocean. Yet, more than sand separates this block of quartz diorite from the sedimentary bulk of northern California: the dunes make manifest to the discerning eye the rift zone of the San Andreas fault.

Geologists speak of California as "tectonically active," but in the early 1960s this part of the state was active in other ways. There were designs on the Head. It had been bored. Now it was ready to receive its crown: a $61 million atomic power plant. With a generation capacity of 325 megawatts, it was to have become the largest nuclear generating station in the United States, the first to cross the threshold of commercial profitability.

But all of this was not to be.

There was strong grassroots opposition to the plans for a reactor at Bodega Head. People worried about the San Andreas fault. The thought of building a nuclear reactor in such a location was unsettling. Although this particular section of the fault is quiet most of the time, during the 1906 quake that devastated San Francisco the ground here shifted a full ten feet. Debate over the issue was intense, but in the end the power company withdrew its application for a license to build and operate a nuclear generating station at Bodega Head. "We would be the last," a 1964 press release assured an increasingly wary public, "to desire to build a plant with any substantial doubt existing as to public safety."

Today Bodega Head is a state park. The "Glory Hole" is a freshwater pond. The scarified land has recovered into a fragrant mosaic of grassland, coyote bush, cow parsnip, and poison oak. The edges of the pond are thick with cattails and rushes. Only a keen landscape sensibility would be able to detect signs of the previous near-plutonic goings-on. Persephone has returned to the daylight, at play once again amid the blooms.

↭

Some years ago I attended a conference on "California Power Places" in the hills above Napa Valley. One session was led by a woman named Lynne. By avocation a horticulturist specializing in California native plants, she made her "real money" as a technical writer for one of the computer companies in the Silicon Valley. Ordinary looking, slightly overweight, Lynne was in her midfifties. She dressed like an old hippie. One got the impression that this was her weekend wardrobe.

The session focused on "spirit of place." The Romans had a term, *genius loci,* to refer to the divinity that resided in a particular locale. The genius of a place—like that of a human—is a higher and more spacious form of presence, whose extent no one quite knows. The goal of our session was to come up with ways that we in the modern world might reestablish contact with these local divinities. "We must be practical," our session leader admonished us, "not theoretical. The spirits are very down-to-earth."

To encourage the group to talk about our own experiences, no matter how strange they might be, Lynne shared a story about an encounter she had with one of those outcrops of chert (locally referred to as "knockers") on the western slopes of Mount Tamalpais. She was walking along through the steep grassland with her friend Bill when she suddenly heard what sounded like voices rising from between the rocks. She felt the need to stop and investigate. Though hearing nothing himself, Bill was used to his companion's endearing eccentricities, so he provided support.

"I'm going down," she announced, and promptly got on hands and knees and—like a dabbling duck dipping in the water—stuck her head down between the rocks, her bottom up toward the sky. The next thing Bill knew, Lynne was flying up and backward, as if tossed. She landed on her butt in the grass. Having suffered no major injury, she did have a slight bruise on her forehead, what looked like a small dent.

"They whacked me!"

"Who whacked you?"

"The spirits in those rocks."

Lynne reported that when she stuck her head between those rocks, she suddenly found herself peering down, as if from the ceiling of a vast cavern, into a realm where shadowy, gnomelike figures were flitting about in a great commotion.

"They were not happy to see me," she explained. "One of them stood underneath me and threw a fist up at my forehead. That sent me right back up into our world."

Blessed with a healthy curiosity, Bill himself investigated the rocks. He found no portal to the underworld, only the solid earth. Yet, he believed Lynne's story. Over the years he had seen her tossed up from other rocks—as well as from stumps, tombstones, and one time an apartment complex Dumpster. Her world was loud with voices that otherwise go unheard. She lent them her ear. Bill, that durable witness, had seen enough of this ordinary woman's extraordinary encounters with the world to have faith in her experience.

Yes, this woman Lynne, who had a normal nine-to-five job and grew flowers on the weekend, was "crazy"—I came away from the session with a profound sense of *that*—but it was a refreshing crazi-ness, one that punctuates day-to-day routine with a sense of wonder. Something blossoms in Lynne that is missing from the corporate, academic, and government worlds that constitute our mainstream culture. She has a playful style of being that does not lay waste to the full human power of perception. She regularly obtains glimpses of things that leave her open to public ridicule and secret envy. She is nuts, though perhaps only on the weekend.

So I told her—why not?—about the time I saw a whole New England graveyard of ghosts leap up from the ground and chase me as I drove my car down an isolated road. I was terrified at the time, not so much of the ghosts but that somehow it would be found out that I saw ghosts. I drove on toward my destination with hasty determination.

"They must have had something important to tell you," Lynne now endeavored to explain. She chastised me for not stopping for those spirits radiating out of the eastern Maine landscape who, for reasons that remain tucked in their graves, wanted to have a word with me.

I came away from that session energized. There amid the live oaks and aromatic laurels of an incandescent October afternoon, I experi-enced a catharsis, I who have spent much of my adult life under the fluorescent lights of the university. For the first time in a long while I felt an alignment between the inner and outer worlds. In the end, can it be said that this woman Lynne is any more crazy than those who would build nuclear power plants along active earthquake faults?

In her journal, the writer Mary Austin described "a sensual way of beholding." When it comes to the land, she insisted that there is "something else there besides what you find in the books; a lurking, evasive Something, wistful, cruel, ardent; something that rustled and ran, that hung half-remotely, insistent on being noticed, fled from pursuit, and when you turned from it, leaped suddenly and fastened on your vitals. This is no mere figure of speech, but the true move-ment of experience." John Muir, the great conservationist and founder of the Sierra Club, occasionally mentions angels in his essays. There is evidence to suggest he was speaking literally.

Our everyday lives and especially our literature are full of kooks, no question about it. Necessary kooks. The kook is a fringe figure, outside any ideology, who is in some way akin to the shamans of old. Mircea Eliade tells us that shamans are the precursors to what we today call poets. All of these crackpots—shamans, poets, pilgrims to California Power Places, and even the nuclear engineers who dream their Promethean dreams—direct our attention to what Eliade describes as "the fabulous world of the gods and magicians, the world in which *everything seems possible,* where the dead return to life and the living die only to live again, where one can disappear and reappear instantaneously, where the 'laws of nature' are abolished, and a certain superhuman 'freedom' is exemplified and made dazzlingly *present*."

These full-souled people living on the edge are neither reasonable nor timid; they are, after all, enthusiasts in the root sense of the word, that is, "filled with a god." In reading our eminently reasonable environmental analyses and histories that come out of the universities and government agencies, the soul in its quest for meaning encounters a debilitating resistance to its progress. No wonder it resorts elsewhere for inspiration. Places like Bodega Head, Yosemite, Yellowstone, or any of our state-sanctioned wilderness areas. Yet, can we say with assurance that even these places serve?

Because it is now "wild" and has a luminous history, Bodega Head serves as a spiritual *locus minoris resistentiae,* a "place of lesser resistance," where all the ghosts and demons who drive each of us around like a tour bus can get out and stretch their legs, leaving the "vehicle"—that is, the ego—parked and emptied. Since you yourself are the vehicle, you ought to be alert to when this emptying out of consciousness occurs, because it is then that you will see just what a heap of trouble you are, this "person" who is amalgamated of so many predilections, untested beliefs, and other moods that if you tried to inventory them you would only get lost for trying. If you don't like the vehicle metaphor, abandon it and call yourself a "spiritual questor," or a "pilgrim to the wild."

The multiplicity of the world is its own compensation. Unaccountable things happen to upset our willful systems—ungovernable occurrences such as dreams, which were so important not only to the

97

shamans that Eliade writes of but also to the ancient Greeks and Romans, who themselves were still close to a shamanistic worldview. Dreams, after all, are the stuff from which pied pipers such as Marx and Freud fashioned their respective lifeworks.

Just before I moved from California I made a pilgrimage to Bodega Head. To see this place today and compare it to the photos taken almost forty years ago gives great encouragement to those who place their faith in "ecological restoration." A beautiful place has been saved; indeed, it has returned to a condition far wilder than it was in the early sixties just before the power company started digging its hole, for in the long decades prior to that the Head had been heavily grazed by horses, cattle, and sheep. The effect of letting all these hungry farm animals loose on the Head was to tear up the soil and eliminate most of the beautiful wildflowers and lupine shrubs. Nowadays the only animals you see here are human, and they graze on the scenery. To judge from the congested campgrounds and the endless conga lines of motor homes on the narrow Coastal Highway, we are just as hungry for beautiful places as sheep are for grass.

At present we are free to walk through this recovered patch of pristine California and meditate deeply upon the awesome natural power inherent in this place. We can indulge our appetite for beauty at Bodega Head State Park because our electricity is being generated in other parts. An economist would call this a "tradeoff." The Greek philosopher Heraclitus says the same thing, albeit with cryptic panache: "The beginning and the end are shared in the circumference of a circle." And Ralph Waldo Emerson, in his essay "Compensation," expresses this fundamental paradox of existence in terms relevant to the case at hand: "To empty here, you must condense there."

The power company, perhaps not totally ignorant of the Great Western Tradition in philosophy, reminded its customers of fateful inevitability when, in language somewhat less polished than Emerson's, they withdrew their application for the power plant at Bodega Head: "We have made provision for adequate electric generating capacity elsewhere to take care of our customers' needs for the several years immediately ahead. Our decision to withdraw the Bodega application does not mean we have lost any confidence whatsoever in nuclear-electric generation."

The power company stood by its words, persevering for more than a decade against strong opposition before finally opening their Diablo Canyon nuclear plant, not far south of California's renowned Big Sur, in a landscape equally spectacular—and tectonically active—as Bodega Head. The Glory Hole on the northern California coast has been filled with water and birdsong; two new glory holes subsequently opened on the central coast have been filled with ingenious machines that split atoms.

Although part of me is disquieted by the thought of the Diablo Canyon plant, I used with gratitude the electricity the power company supplied when I lived in California, and I always paid my bills on time. The company would occasionally print a message at the bottom of my monthly bill: "We appreciate the opportunity to serve you. Your payment history establishes you as a good credit customer. Thank you." I take this to mean we have good relations, myself and this corporation. If both Artemis and Reddy Kilowatt are among the pantheon of gods that cavort in the hearts of late-twentieth-century Americans, you can't very well build an altar to the one and not expect to incur the wrath of the other.

After my visit to Bodega Head, a dream came to me. It goes like this: *I am standing on the edge of the pond that once was the "Glory Hole." Its waters sparkle with sunlight. From atop the cattails and rushes, red-winged blackbirds call out to each other. Suddenly a giant humanlike figure begins to rise, head first, from the water. The head is monstrously large and out of proportion to the body. Atop the water the figure now stands, covered with mud. Swallows are stitching innumerable circles in the air around the figure's very big head. Suddenly the swallows transmogrify into dark and fast-moving cumulus nimbus clouds; they gather furiously. Sparks begin to issue in the air around the figure's head. The whole world darkens and heavy rain falls. The mud is washed away, revealing the figure to be none other than that trademark of the power industry, Reddy Kilowatt. He is smiling—or is it laughing? Gone is the Glory Hole, all of this now taking place in a vast electrical switchyard right out of my New Jersey childhood, when my father worked for the power company. Overhead in the dark sky is an infernal grid of transmission lines, on the horizon nothing but transmission towers. A voice says: "It's a risk worth taking; all of this is beautiful."* I awaken with tears.

Ethnographers nearly a century ago reported that, among some of the Indian peoples of northern California, a man or woman became a shaman only after dreaming at home of the spirits. At that point, the dreamer could call in a doctor, who was usually an elder relative, in order to obtain his or her "spirit heritage"—that is, receive instruction for right conduct with these beings. Or the dreamer could go at once to the mountains to seek and appease the spirits who had come for a visit.

I dreamed my dream at home, long after my visit to the coast. I have no relatives who are shamans; the only doctors I know are M.D.'s and Ph.D.'s. I suppose I could have gone to the mountains— or back to Bodega Head—to appease the spirit who came to me as Reddy Kilowatt, but I believe the dream was telling me I had to search elsewhere. I won't find Reddy Kilowatt in those wilderness places our lawmakers define as "untrammeled by man." Such places are already overcrowded with our romantic ideas if not ourselves. Perhaps instead I need to go to Diablo Canyon in California, or to the Yard's Creek Generating Station in New Jersey, or to Yucca Mountain in Nevada. Somehow I don't think any of this is quite right either.

"Show me Thy glory!" Moses shouted to his god from the wilderness area atop Mount Sinai. Now other gods are begging our attention. No need to shout. They too have their glory, and they are near at hand.

LIFE AT THE CAULDRON

JUST AFTER SUNRISE ON A DAY IN MAY NOT LONG AGO, IN A HOT-SPRING pool near the South Fork of Idaho's Payette River, a man's body was found floating facedown in the water. He had been shot once in the head. The incident occurred in the middle of nowhere, so police investigators had a long drive to get there. Little evidence was recovered at the crime scene: no eyewitnesses, no signs of a scuffle, no bloody footprints leading away from the body. Police did talk with some kayakers staying at a nearby Forest Service campground. They had been down at the hot spring on the previous evening as late as eight o'clock. No body there then. Now there was, and the kayakers were upset. This was the wilderness, they said; things like this aren't supposed to happen here.

The police bound off the area around the hot spring with a yellow plastic ribbon. "We're setting up a perimeter," an officer explained. The onlookers nodded their approval. Printed on the yellow ribbon in black letters was a message, "Police Crime Scene—Do Not Cross." The message was repeated continuously along the length of the ribbon. It went on for more than a hundred yards. Since this was a perimeter, the ribbon came back upon itself and formed a rough circle on the landscape; the message became a kind of infinite loop. The onlookers took comfort in seeing police authority stretched around such a tainted scene. The order of things had suffered a deep gash, but now a tourniquet was firmly in place.

The investigation proceeded. There were indications that the man had been killed right in the hot-spring pool. He had identification on him but no money. How he wound up in the pool, who killed him, and why were formidable mysteries. It was as if, standing at the bottom of some colossal billboard, you looked up and tried to make sense of it. The upper parts would appear smaller and the lower larger than they should, while all of the colors and lines would swirl in clouds of confusion. The totality of the image does not reveal itself to one standing too close—only backing off will bring the big picture into focus. Could be that it's a man hanging miserably on a cross, or perhaps an oversized Guernsey wanting to know if you've got milk, or maybe it's an extratall circus clown peddling hamburgers. In any case, when it comes to a mystery, achieving the proper vantage point is critical.

The first break in the case came a few days later when an abandoned car was found in the city. A blue Ford Escort. Somebody had parked it behind two huge Dumpsters in a hotel lot, not easy to see. "Whoever was driving that car knew it was hot and stashed it," said the cop who found it. In the weeds along the edge of the parking lot, investigators discovered a crumpled bumper sticker. It said, "I Believe in Dragons, Good Men and Mystical Things." It had been taped in the rear window of the Escort, and somebody had removed it. A detective said, "That bumper sticker was taken from the car, thrown in the Dumpster, and the wind blew it out."

As it happens, both Escort and bumper sticker belonged to the dead man. When the police searched his apartment for evidence, they found among his effects a number of books on marketing strategy, customer behavior, and witchcraft—as well as a strange homemade mirror, the surface of which was painted jet-black. It reflected nothing. "What the hell is this?" asked the cop who discovered it. Nobody could say. They took it away to the police evidence warehouse, along with anything else that might have some bearing on the case. Fingerprints other than the victim's were found all over the apartment, and they matched sets taken from the car. The pieces of the puzzle quickly fell into place. Soon two suspects were in custody. Over the next few days, more details were flushed from cover, and a story unfolded in the newspapers. It went something like this.

The dead man's name was Kelvin. He was twenty-nine years old and had been studying marketing communications at the university in Boise. He lived in an apartment close to campus. Although raised in the Mormon church, he had since become enchanted by other things. In the months prior to his death, he had been studying witchcraft, but not at the university—he was receiving private instruction. Names were never revealed.

People who lived in Kelvin's apartment building described him as somebody they didn't really know. He was a discrete character; nothing in his world seemed to overlap with anything in theirs. One of his fellow citizens—you couldn't really call them "neighbors," as the only interest they held in common was that the city remove their trash once a week—told a television news reporter: "There was something strange about him. I can't describe it. People come and go and that's pretty much it."

On that night in May, Kelvin drove his car from Boise into the mountains. He was accompanied by two young men in their late teens. News accounts gratuitously referred to them as "transients," but they were friends of the victim and well known around town. The two young men each had a long record of petty theft and writing bad checks. Kelvin somehow befriended them, even though he himself had never stolen anything or written a bad check in his life. His mother described him as "a good-hearted man."

He often drove the two young men around in his car because they didn't have one. Together they ate a lot of fast food and smelled like it. Sometimes he would let them stay with him in his apartment. The three were part of a larger group caught up in Dungeons and Dragons, a role-playing game that skirts the line between fantasy and reality. At some point, Kelvin told the two young men about his witchcraft studies and showed them his magic mirror. They were fascinated.

One day in the midst of a Dungeons and Dragons game, the two young men noticed a receipt lying around Kelvin's apartment. It was for an eight-thousand-dollar student loan. The two young men figured this was a lot of money, so they decided to steal it. The only question was, how? The money was in Kelvin's bank account, and they needed a plan to get at it. The magic mirror was lying nearby, so they consulted it—perhaps in the hope of finding a co-conspirator among the disembodied—but they couldn't get it to work. Then the two young men noticed that Kelvin kept a couple of hunting rifles in his closet; these became part of the plan. Things grew apace, like cheat grass across the western range.

Here's what they came up with. They would lure Kelvin to a remote area, force him at gunpoint to give over the access code to his bank account, and then kill him. Afterward, they would return to the city and withdraw the cash. "This was their way," a detective put it. "They were going to split it four thousand dollars each." The two young men were deep into a new game.

Around ten on that fateful night, they suggested to Kelvin that they all drive up to the hot spring. It was an odd hour for such things, but for some reason Kelvin was drawn to the idea. You might say that at this point his life had become a deep basin of strange attractions. There are those who say that he just didn't pay enough attention to evil—for if he had, he never would have spent time with these guys. Experience would suggest there are certain souls that are like cheap motels where all kinds of atrocities find ready lodging, and here were two young men with "No Vacancy" signs burning in their eyes.

They all got into the car and headed north. Their destination lay more than an hour's drive through the dark woods of Idaho. High mountains added to the darkness. By the time they arrived at the hot-spring parking lot, the waning moon was struggling to rise over a barren ridge—just enough light to make out the long descent of stone steps to the hot-spring pool. Kelvin led the way. Although he had never been to this place before, it seemed strangely familiar. The ponderosa pine made the night air smell like an ice cream cone. A coyote barked in the distance. The river churned through the gorge below.

Kelvin didn't notice anything was wrong until he was sitting comfortably in the warmth of the hot spring. Only then did he see two sinister images reflected in the black waters of the pool—a couple of bad ideas suddenly manifesting in the mind of God—and each one pointing a rifle at the image of Kelvin's head. Had he attended carefully to the semblances in the mirrored waters, he could have witnessed the terror blossoming in his own eyes like a pair of phantom orchids.

The jaw of one of the images started moving up and down as if to speak. It was like a dream. Kelvin heard a voice demanding the access code to his bank account. The voice seemed far away, as if coming from the moon. Kelvin pleaded with the images for his life. He gave them what they asked. It wasn't enough. A sudden flash and the whole reflection shattered, as if something heavy had just been dropped into it.

↭

When the two young men got back to the city they discovered that Kelvin had given them the wrong access code. Now there wouldn't be any money. They were really angry and they cursed their victim savagely, revealing the truth in the old saying that offenders never forgive. In their rage, they ditched the car but forgot to wipe it for fingerprints. Soon after they were in jail. Even though both confessed to plotting the crime, it's not clear which one actually killed Kelvin. Only one shot was fired, but each young man accused the other of pulling the trigger. The rifles had been thrown into the river and were never recovered.

The newspapers kept hinting at something strange about this case. It started to come out during the preliminary hearing when the prosecution asked the sixteen-year-old wife of one of the two young men if her husband was into witchcraft. She replied, "From my understanding, he was into . . ." She never completed her thought because her husband's attorney objected to the question. He knew a Pandora's box when he saw one. The judge sustained the objection. There was already plenty of evidence to bind the two young men over for trial.

↭

As more details of the Hot Springs Murder (that's what the newspapers were calling it) came to light that spring, especially those pertaining to witchcraft and magic mirrors, I found myself reflecting on my undergraduate days at the University of Maine. It was a time when weirdness hung in the air thicker than the pot smoke in the dormitory hallways. I was taking a class on horror literature from the writer Stephen King, and for a term project I decided to spend a night in a haunted house. All I had to do was find one.

I heard about a place down in Bar Harbor, so I went to investigate. Although there were lots of stories about this house—most of them involving a headless sea captain come back to claim a hatbox full of love letters—finding the place proved more difficult than catching its ghost. People would say things like, "I hear talk of that house, but I've never actually been there myself," or "Oh, yeah, I was there once in high school, but it was at night and I was with a bunch of friends and we were kind of drunk. I think it was over by Otter Creek, but that might be some other place." And a surprising number of people in town seemed to have the same "friend of a friend," an intrepid fellow who tried to spend a night in this house but was chased out by a ghostly set of limbs and a torso that suddenly appeared and then tumbled down the steps, as if spilled from a children's toy chest or something, only to assemble at the bottom as the headless sea captain, which then gave chase to the fellow, who fled the scene and indeed the town of Bar Harbor, for he had not been spotted there since, though his hair is said to have turned white for the experience and that's how you will know him if you ever run into him.

Over the course of my inquiries, one name kept coming up as somebody who might be able to help. "Go see Melissa," they said. "If anybody knows where that house is, she does." As I soon discovered, this Melissa was a woman my age who was "into" witchcraft, her specialty being the manufacture of magic mirrors. This may seem an odd occupation nowadays, maybe even a little quaint, but it was the sort of thing you did in Maine back in the seventies if you didn't own a big summer "cottage" and you had gotten tired of working as a laborer in the gardens and country clubs of the rich or as a deckhand on their yachts. It was either that, or you married one of them, or you robbed their places in the winter. There just weren't many options.

Melissa had a little shop in downtown Bar Harbor, so I stopped in for a chat. I got to know her somewhat over the next few weeks. She had hair the color of a fire bush in the fall, and she wore long flowing dresses all the time and shoes hardly ever. It was a look that in college we called "organic." You could almost see the bits of granola shaking out from the folds of her peasant skirt as she walked down the street, or imagine the little flock of birds following in her train feeding on what bits of fruit and nuts might be gleaned. "Watch out, O'Grady," my friend Westphal warned me when I told him I had been speaking with her. He had gone to high school with her and knew something of her history.

Tradition had it that, on her mother's side, Melissa was descended from a woman who was executed in the Salem witch trials. This curious bit of family lore—no ordinary skeleton in the closet—had been a great source of embarrassment to Melissa while she was growing up, but in college she took a course in women's studies from Professor Phoebe, who convinced her that witches are an oppressed minority. Having a genuine Salem witch-hunt victim for an ancestor could be a fabulous boon, the professor convinced her, so Melissa embraced her heritage and turned it into a business.

She dropped out of college and opened a shop and called it "Mirror, Mirror on the Wall." She sold nothing but genuine magic mirrors, each of which she made herself. Assembling them was an elaborate process, requiring carpentry skills and lots of time and labor, plus it all had to be done at night when the moon was waxing—this is it what endowed the mirrors with a special power. Finally, according to what I heard, each mirror had to be "jump-started" by being dipped in a certain tide pool in Acadia National Park at midnight when the moon was in Pisces, an aspect of production that, had the Park Service known about it, would have led if not to Melissa's persecution than certainly her prosecution. Park Service administrators have an aversion to occult practices taking place anywhere on government property. Such goings-on, they declare, stigmatize the resource.

So there I was in the witch's shop, with its abundance of strange mirrors hanging on the wall, each one looking like a blemish on the face of all things bright and reasonable. Trying to hide my discomfort, I introduced myself and casually asked about the haunted house and its headless sea captain. The witch laughed at me.

"Don't you believe in ghosts?" I asked.

She laughed again, and said she had seen far too many to believe in them. "That's just a story," she added, with a hint of that pity usually reserved for the easily duped. Meanwhile, my term project was vanishing faster than its ghost.

"Well, then, tell me about these mirrors," I said. "How are they supposed to work if you can't see anything in them?"

The witch explained that these were *magic* mirrors, not for ordinary eyes but only for those who wish to delve beneath the surface of things. Each magic mirror, she assured me, was a kind of mental door into a marvelous world.

She lifted a handheld mirror from behind the counter. "Here," she said, "try for yourself. Think of it as a gate for your mind to go through. When it opens, you'll have a way to get out of your normal life." Melissa, as I quickly came to realize, regarded ordinary consciousness as something that needed to be escaped. For her, the word *normal* had all the connotations of Alcatraz.

For my part, I had concerns about doors like this. If they're locked, I figure it's usually for good reason. But at that point, time was running out for my research project, and I needed something to replace the haunted house. I thought maybe I could write something about these magic mirrors. Later, when I ran the idea by Steve King, he was all for it—he already knew enough about haunted houses and was game for a look into other things.

Nervously, I accepted the mirror from Melissa and had a look-see. Nothing. "What am I doing wrong?"

She was more than willing to set me aright. There is a part of the mind—she called it a third eye—that once opened can see the images that dwell deep in the magic mirror. Everybody knows that a mirror is supposed to reflect things, but less apparent is its capacity to *absorb* the images it captures. The dull black surface of a magic mirror reflects nothing; the point of this opacity is to make it easier to draw forth the images that have already been lodged away in there. Think of it, the mirror in your bathroom or in your car, the storefront glass you pass on the way to work, even your beloved's eyes—all these are not just hurling back the accidental rays of your sweet self, but also soaking them in. An image cast into a mirror is like a deposit in some spectacular treasury, a veritable Fort Knox of the soul—something like memory itself. Not only that, but also each mirror is linked to every other mirror—past, present, and future—so that by having an "account" in one, you actually have access to all the others, something along the lines of a vast banking network that cuts across space and time. The magic mirror is your passbook.

A few days later when I returned to the shop for a "mirror session," Melissa sat me down at a small table in a dimly lit back room. She set a mirror—"I chose it specially for you"—in a small tripod on the table. "Concentrate," she said. "Gaze into the mirror. Don't be filled with distractions. Take time. Relax. Empty your mind. Look at it. Look through it. Let it open up. Have no expectations, no demands, no agenda. Take time. Relax. Empty your mind." Then she left me alone with all that emptiness, closing the door behind her.

↭

What I've concluded in the years since is that a magic mirror, in the broadest sense, is really any object whose surface lends itself as a projection screen for the unconscious. That means just about anything will do. Most assuredly, the world itself is a magic mirror, which includes your family, your house, your car, your religion, your job, all the grudges you harbor, the ambitions you nurture, the games you like to play and the games you like to watch, as well as that empty beer can somebody tossed on your lawn last night. It also includes the old woman in the supermarket aisle who, finding all the cereal boxes too big, shouts to no one: "Don't they know millions of us live alone? How can I eat all these corn flakes by myself?!"

As to be expected, the permeable style of consciousness cultivated by habitual use of magic mirrors has its drawbacks. Melissa admitted that she had become so adept at seeing images in her magic mirror that she now saw them in all kinds of inappropriate places like swimming pools and glasses of water in restaurants. There were some days when she could hardly bring herself to walk down the street for all the house windows glaring at her. When I asked her why she didn't just flip off those unsolicited images, she said, "It's never wise to be rude to them—they react maliciously."

And sure enough my session caused me a few problems of my own, even though I was never able to see anything in the mirror. That night I had a disturbing dream, which recurred for the next three after that.

In the dream, I'm standing outside a huge redbrick slaughterhouse in Sioux Falls, South Dakota, or someplace like it. There's a high-pitched whine coming from inside the building that sounds like a hundred giant band saws all going at once. I don't see them, but I know that inside the slaughterhouse are thousands upon thousands of trembling cows being herded, one by one, to their bloody band-saw deaths. Outside where I am it's sunset, and suddenly a dark swarm of bees, thick as an inversion layer of mortuary smoke, comes rushing in from the bleeding horizon to blot out what remains of the sun. But when the swarm gets closer, I see it's not bees but a huge flock of passenger pigeons buzzing like bees, and they start gathering over the redbrick slaughterhouse, thicker and thicker, until, one by one, each bird bursts into a ball of fire. Meanwhile, inside the slaughterhouse, cows continue to be herded, one by one, and for each cow that dies, a passenger pigeon explodes in flammable witness. Always at that point I woke up.

I told Melissa about this dream and asked her if it had anything to do with the magic mirror. She said not to worry—it was just a warm-up for bigger things. Steve King, on the other hand, suggested caution, casually mentioning that spirits are known to flock to sacrifice because they feed on spilled blood. "Maybe something *bad* came through that mirror and now you're dreaming about it. I'd watch it if I were you."

Oh, I didn't like any of this. Right then, I swore I would never look into another magic mirror. And just to play it safe, I became a vegetarian. That was more than twenty years ago; I've stuck to it and haven't had the dream again.

Today when people ask me why I don't eat meat, they presume it's a moral decision. Usually I tell them I just don't like the stuff, that it's a matter of taste, not morality. I don't tell them my real reason for avoiding flesh: *fear.* I also don't mention how I bypass the butcher section in supermarkets like some people steer clear of "bad neighbor-hoods," or how, when I'm driving down the neon thoroughfare of America, I make sure not to stop or even look too long at all those McDonalds and Wendy's and Burger Kings—for fear of what I might see swarming through the grease clouds that billow from the kitchen vents on the rooftops and spin off in ghostly threads to attach like phantom lampreys to cars that pass through the Horned Gate of the drive-through. I never mention these matters. Philosophical talk about the nature of sacrifice is best avoided in polite company.

⊸⊝

One night, a few weeks after Kelvin's body was found, a Forest Service ranger noticed some strange goings-on down at the hot spring. He decided to investigate. When he descended the stone steps to the pool, he found candles burning everywhere and a dozen or so men and women standing holding hands in a ring around the hot spring. They were all naked. In and of itself, nudity at a hot spring is nothing uncommon, but these people were chanting while one of them dangled a mirror from a string over the pool. The forest ranger thought this suspicious. When he confronted them, they said they were doing a "working."

"What's a working?" the forest ranger wanted to know.

The naked people stood quietly for a moment. A couple of them shuffled their bare feet. The candlelight flickered on their bodies. Then one of them said the soul of the man killed here was trapped in the pool. They were using the mirror to catch and release it.

The forest ranger told them they had to break it up.

⊸⊝

Since timber production in Idaho has fallen off considerably in recent years and most of the mills are now closed, the U.S. Forest Service is trying to redefine itself. Recreation is replacing wood as the main product coming from the public lands, and the agency is investing a lot of money into its "interpretive programs." That means lots of new signs—or "signage," as they like to say—are being put up at the more popular sites such as reservoir beaches and hot springs.

So if you visit a particular hot spring near the South Fork of the Payette River, you'll find some big new signs in the parking lot. They tell you about "Life at the Cauldron." On good authority you will learn that the flora and fauna associated with the hot-spring environ- ment is "supported here but not elsewhere." If, during your "hot spring adventure," you look around carefully, you might spot the narrow-winged damselfly (sometimes called "fire-breeding dragon"), or

111

you could see the hot springs snail, or the soldier fly, or maybe some panic grass. If you're really lucky you might encounter a "rare orchid that in Idaho only grows near hot springs."

The signs, however, say very little about the most common species found around here, whose highly visible traces include empty beer cans, stumps of candles, and soiled underwear tangled in the artemisia shrubs. About the only thing you will learn in regard to human beings is that "Some early settlers in this region believed that such hot, smelly water associated with the spring escaped from the 'hellish' interior of the earth."

If you come to this place hoping to learn more about the Hot Springs Murder, you will be disappointed. The signs in the parking lot say nothing about it. Nobody you ask in the campground will know anything. You may see a couple of overturned trash cans and some garbage strewn about—the work of a local bear—but you won't find any remnants of yellow plastic ribbon. The long descent of stone steps may seem familiar, but you won't know why. When you get to the bottom, you will find nothing telltale about the hot spring itself. And if, at last, you take a long, deep look into the river, now settled into the placid flows of late summer, you may see your own reflection scudding along amid the eddies, but these waters will not give up their secrets.

You could stop in at the U.S. Forest Service information station a couple miles down the road and make some inquiries, but don't expect to be received warmly. The Forest Service wants to manage the interpretation of the forest in the same strict and scientific way they used to manage for timber. Unregulated stories such as the Hot Springs Murder are like bark beetles or forest fires, a counterproductive side of nature that is best eradicated or brought under control. When a forest ranger talks about rumors spreading like wildfire, you can bet he is not just speaking metaphorically.

I stopped in myself at the Forest Service to obtain a little information. The ranger was happy to provide me with all kinds of materials pertaining to the hydrology of hot springs and the best locations for parking my RV if I had one. He spoke glowingly of all the "recreational opportunities" on the National Forest, and he generously offered to tell me where the best fishing holes were. He was wearing a ranger hat and doing a good job.

Then I said, "So, what's this I hear about naked witches down at the hot spring?"

It was an inappropriate question. He shook his head grimly and looked at me as if I had committed a crime. Then he said, "It's a real shame that resource has become stigmatized." And sent me on my way.

THE GENIUS OF KAATERSKILL FALLS

A LOCAL LEGEND HAS IT THAT IF YOU STAND AT THE BRINK OF KAATERSKILL
Falls when the light of the moon is just right and gaze down at a
particular flat-topped boulder in the middle of the creek, you can see
her sitting there still, a pale-blue luminescence. How many people
have actually glimpsed her is not at all clear—stories of this kind are
notoriously elusive, flitting in and out of certainty, perhaps borne on
the same current as our moods and our memory. You can say that she
is something like true love: often talked about but seldom met in real
life. Nevertheless, you may wish to investigate this matter for yourself.

Go then to Kaaterskill Falls, which is in the Catskill Mountains of
New York, not far from where Rip Van Winkle took his twenty-year
nap and dreamed his twenty-year dream. I could draw you a map, but
how reliable would it be? The best places are never found on a chart.

In early-nineteenth-century America, just as the Puritan heaven was
giving way to modern destination resorts, Kaaterskill Falls entered the
popular imagination. The painters painted it and the poets versified it,
then the lovers descended on the place, as they would in later years
on the less lofty Niagara, to gain something for themselves of the
artists' inspiration, to witness the water's twisting surrender to the air,
its rapid and bewildering passage from above to below. Ah, but that
was long ago, and the place is nearly forgotten today. There isn't even
a sign posted for it anymore.

During the Kaaterskill's heyday, a wily entrepreneur—operating on the principle of "You get what you pay for"—built a dam on the creek just above the falls so he could control the stream flow. If you wanted to make a splash with your date, now you had to give the gatekeeper a quarter to "turn on the falls." Almost nobody objected to this arrangement, perhaps because in those days it was still believed that art improved nature. Nevertheless, there are always a few scofflaws who resist the commercial mitigation of the wild heart.

In this case it was an enthusiastic suitor who knew that a fetching landscape would fetch him his love, so he brought her to Kaaterskill Falls. He didn't have much money, and he resented having to pay for the privilege of pitching his woo, so he devised a plan to steal some water that he might steal a kiss. One summer night when the moon was full and nobody was guarding the dam, the young suitor led his unchaperoned darling through the forest to the base of the falls and set her up on a flat-topped boulder in the middle of the creek. She was wearing a blue wool dress. He could see the moon in her eyes, and in that moon he could see his own image reflected. Unfortunately, the dam on the stream above had reduced the falls to a mossy dribble, hardly commensurate with the young suitor's exuberance. He was in love! Where was the torrent he required? This was supposed to be a wild place where you might do wild things. Everything about the moment seemed to say: "Show me your love!"

So the young suitor left his love in her blue wool dress, scrambled up the steep and thickly wooded side of the canyon, and made his way to the dam above the falls. Everything was still. Behind the dam was a lovely lake, and it reflected the lovely moon. For a moment or two, he pondered the stillness of the lake, and the stillness of the moon in the lake, and the stillness of his own image in the moon in the lake. Then he threw open the gates. Wide open.

The waters, so placid just a moment ago, let loose in a furious rush. The surge was a surprise. The roar was terrific. Things emptied out more quickly than he had anticipated. Although the moon in the sky held its place, the moon in the lake was swept over the brink by the freshet this man had set free. He could hear the horrific flood making its way down the canyon, scouring out the stream channel, uprooting ancient trees and tossing boulders untossed since passage of the last glacier. This deluge, now booming, now crashing, now fading away in the valley below, dissolved at last into the night. Silence returned. Gone was the artificial lake, and gone its genuine beauty. In its wake, a vast and unsavory meadow of mud, unredeemable even by the light of the moon. Below the falls lay havoc unimaginable.

In a panic now, the young suitor thrashed his way back through the dark forest and down the steep side of the canyon to the spot where he had left his love. She was gone. The boulder itself had shifted some thirty feet down from where he remembered it. A tangle of fallen trees was lodged against its upstream side. Everything was dripping with mud. He shouted her name. Only the echo returned.

During the next several days the distraught young man combed the dangerous watercourse downstream from the falls, but could find no trace of the girl. Some say she got tired of waiting for her ardent date, so she simply walked off in annoyance. Others say she was swept to her death by the flood, and now her ghost, enshrouded in what appears to be a blue wool dress, haunts the base of the falls in the vicinity of a particular flat-topped boulder. Of the young suitor himself, no further word save that, before he went away in despair too deep to be fathomed, he chiseled the silhouette of his lost love into the rock near the lip of the falls, a graven image that remains visible to this day.

As for that pale-blue luminescence that can be seen when the light of the moon is just right, there are those who insist it is only an *ignis fatuus,* a "foolish fire" sought by painters, poets, and kooks who would seduce us away from the facts. I have seen it once or twice myself. It is the genius of Kaaterskill Falls, which is to say that higher and more spacious form of presence whose extent nobody quite knows. Every place, like every human being, has such a genius, though it can be very difficult to discern. Those who do not expect it will not find it, for it is trackless and forever wild.

But as I said, this is a local legend. The story is authentic. Either this or something like it.

THE WEATHER COMING OFF ALL THINGS

PERHAPS THE PAST *IS* INTERRED IN THE PRESENT, AS SOME HAVE MAIN-
tained, and the world is its own enduring monument. Material objects
thus possess an inner or spiritual life, just as human beings do, and
these things have their own memories, fully capable of being transmit-
ted or passed along to one open to such impressions. Nobody would
deny something like this is the case with words, those veritable
graveyards of meaning, wherein every tomb lies a Lazarus waiting to
be called forth. Why shouldn't the same be true of material objects?
At least they observe a kind of etiquette, most of the time, and don't
force themselves upon us like some drunk with a story down at the
Jolly-O Tavern. Indeed, the things that compose our world are not so
rude as to speak directly, nor so coy as to conceal vital knowledge,
but instead they give signs. Just like the weather.

On the other hand, there are some people upon whom even the
most trifling of objects will advance like an emotional thunderstorm.
For instance, my old friend Amy Ursi, the New Jersey psychic. Just as
some people can feel in their bones the approach of an oncoming
storm, so she responds in her gut to the atmospheric conditions she
says surround material objects. Each one is enveloped by a mysterious
vapor of presence, the kind of thing said to come up around graves or
in dreams when the beloved dead come back to visit. By her account,
this strange mist is borne aloft from the multitude of things, as if by

winds, to form clouds that circulate in broad patterns across the landscape of the human heart. Lest you take this as a mere figure of speech, I hasten to add that Amy has a stormy temperament. I tend to take her at her word.

Now when it comes to weather in the ordinary sense, meteorologists look at a wide range of phenomena, everything from the jet stream right down to the dust devil swirling across your supermarket parking lot. They use highly sensitive instruments to compile data on minute changes in temperature, air pressure, and humidity. All of this is fed into computers, digested by highly sophisticated programs, then squeezed out in new and presumably more useful forms. These tokens are then "read" by the meteorologists to provide a forecast for your morning commute. Such predictions, shrouded in the same glamorous computer graphics favored by sportscasters, more often than not prove unreliable, yet they somehow suffice to win our confidence. You could say that when it comes to our mental possessions, the wrong ideas are preferable to none.

My old friend Amy is a kind of meteorologist of the soul. Because she is self-taught in these matters, her style of talking about them is more colorful than what passes on the nightly news. She has no degree in atmospheric science, nor does she employ any fancy computer modeling; her instruments of choice are astrology and numerology. For her, the air is filled with all manner of unseen angel, demon, and disembodied soul, which—at least by her reckoning—should come as no surprise, since the air itself is invisible yet nobody doubts it is there. When skeptics challenge her, she just cites the Chandogya Upanishad: "Like the wind, like the clouds, like thunder and lightning, all of which arise from space without physical shape and reach the light in their own form, so too those who rise above ordinary perception ascend to the light in their own form." Obscure as Amy can sometimes sound, when it comes to the things themselves she speaks clearly enough: "Be careful what you handle—there's a forecast in every touch."

Amy has the ability to "tune in" to objects, a curious knack she acquired when we were still in high school. During our senior year, she worked as a retail clerk up at the old EJ Korvettes in West Orange. Not long on the job, she realized she could tell, just by its feel, whether a customer's check was going to bounce. "It sets off this strange buzzing in my ear," I remember her saying. Turned out she was right every time, which much pleased her supervisors. They quickly promoted her to "Store Check Approval Officer," a position created just for her. The modest pay raise and enhanced prestige, such as could be had in those days at EJ Korvettes, were enough to convince Amy that she—the only person from our very large graduating class to get into Princeton—really didn't need to go to college. Instead, she embarked on an "alternative" career in psychic detection, which, when compared to the professions of our classmates—bankers, real estate developers, Hollywood actors, corporate headhunters, and politicians—seems far less wrongheaded than it once did.

Nowadays, of course, computer networks have pretty much killed the need for any extrasensory form of check clearing, but lucky for Amy her clairvoyant abilities extend well beyond the cash register. Give her a photograph of somebody she doesn't know, and you'll see what I mean. She puts it up to her forehead and after a few moments of "incubating the images in the henhouse of her mind"—at least that's how one debunkers' magazine described her methods—she provides a detailed account of events from the life of the person in the photo, such as when a broken arm, when a first kiss, when a parent's death, and even, on a good day, when that individual's own death. Amy has a similar flair when it comes to letters and, of late, e-mail, though she prefers to scan these messages in hard copy rather than press her brow against the monitor. She's also pretty good at "smelling ghosts," able to tell—just by walking in the door and taking a whiff—if your house is haunted.

Amy is fond of saying that a person's breath is just a highly localized form of weather, worthy of at least a little mention on the nightly news if not its own cable channel. In her way of speaking, weather is an allegory for the soul. Sometimes I think she's right—as on one summer afternoon when I stepped out of a Center City Philadelphia movie theater into a furious rainstorm. The whole atmosphere had a greenish pall to it, and the water in the street was running deeper than the city's political grudges. I looked up at the sky just in time to see a dark funnel cloud casually making its way eastward, directly above the buildings along Chestnut Street, as if it were just another tourist from Kansas or Oklahoma come to see the Liberty Bell.

At the same instant I observed two young men not far down the street, engaged in a bitter dispute. They were yelling at each other. One of them abruptly pulled out a knife and plunged it into the thigh of the other, then ran off down a dismal side street, out of sight. The bewildered victim was left hurling curses up into the air as he tried to tend his wound. But then somewhere deep in the recesses of his mind, the idea took hold that he should give chase to his assailant—so he gave up trying to staunch the flow of his blood onto the sidewalk, and instead limped off, to the best of his diminished ability, still hurling curses up into the air, yet making slow progress toward retribution, until he too disappeared down that same dismal side street.

Later that evening, the television news reported a tornado had touched down on the other side of the Delaware River, causing a bit of damage over in Camden but no injuries. What happens in New Jersey is big news. Yet, over here in the City of Brotherly Love it was just another ordinary day—no mention of any stabbing, no report of a washed-out trail of blood and where it might have led. Instead, the fluffy-haired news anchor told us to stay tuned for tomorrow's forecast.

You've probably heard the stories about police departments that use psychics to help crack the really tough cases. Amy is one of the people they call. Contrary to public opinion, the cops don't have a problem with using paranormal methods to solve crimes. On the whole, they are without superstition but not without belief. Since they are pragmatists, they welcome aid from wherever it comes. And Amy always comes through.

Several years ago, an article appeared in one of those check-stand tabloids on the subject of "Psychic Investigators." Amy was just starting out and got some good press here. The article quoted an unnamed Bayonne police detective who had high praise for her abilities: "She hit it right on the head—I mean, I was there when she did it. I don't believe in any of this psychic crap, for the most part, but I think she does have a gift. I've been on this job for a long time and seen a lot of people claiming special powers, but I think Amy comes closest. I found her the most accurate of all of them when it comes to this business."

The case involved the murder of a telemarketing tycoon—or at least the evidence pointed that way—but no corpse had turned up, and the investigation was going nowhere. Having come to their wits' end, the cops brought in Amy. Since she does command a hefty fee, I've often wondered how they report such a charge on their expense forms. I suppose the word *consultation* is versatile enough. In contemporary usage it covers all manner of services rendered, everything from oracles to lawyers, prostitutes to anesthesiologists.

Anyway, the cops handed over to their psychic the one piece of crime scene evidence they had—a small bit of bone believed to have come from the victim. They asked Amy to describe the person and where the rest of the body might be found. The article then recounted how she picked up the bone, pressed it to her forehead, and suddenly screamed out: "A rat! It's a rat! All I can see is this enormous rat in front of my eyes and it's coming right at me! What's going on, did you guys give me the wrong bone?"

Oh no, the cops assured her, that was the right bone all right, definitely human. "Listen, Amy," they said, "the rat you're seeing was probably what chewed the bone off the hand of the victim in the first place, before the killer was able to transport the body. That's what you're picking up. Take another look. Could you just go past that rat and tell us if you see the victim?" So that's what Amy did. Not only was she able to describe the victim, but she also told the cops exactly where the body lay, out there in the Jersey Meadowlands. They took it from there.

If all such cases went as smoothly as this, every police department would keep a psychic on staff full-time. Unfortunately, big problems arise when a "medium" is brought in, whether by the cops or by somebody who's just in an emotional crisis. Not that a true psychic will fail to "pick up on the vibes" in any case, but they often pick up on the *wrong* vibes. When it comes to perception, if you make your mind as hospitable to vagrant images as these psychics do, then you're exposing yourself to some pretty chancy stuff. They say it's like walking out of a dark cave into the bright light of an afternoon, or worse, staring directly into the sun to watch an eclipse: your eyes fill up with darkness and you're left groping around blindly. This is just a metaphor, but when something like this happens to a psychic, it's a major embarrassment for all concerned.

Like any sensitive seer, Amy occasionally locks on to information that, well, isn't exactly related to the case. Such as the time she was working with an elephant figurine. She blithely supplied her police audience with a wealth of lurid details about a ménage à trois that she was picking up on, a little drama somebody later described as a "pornographic Nancy Drew Meets the Hardy Boys." As the titillating scene was being fleshed out by Amy, the detective who had handed her the evidence in the first place began to fidget. You could see the thunderheads of anxiety building up over his head, until all attention in the room was on him.

Then suddenly—Boom!—he jumps up and puts a halt to the proceedings. "This is going nowhere," he blurts out as he snatches the figurine back from Amy and bolts from the room, leaving his fellow detectives—with one or two nervous exceptions—snickering in delight.

For her part, Amy has cultivated a degree of circumspection unrivaled in her field. As she once told a reporter, "I try not to tune in to the X-rated stuff. The police worry that I'm going to see things about their sex life or about who they went out with last night or who they're cheating on. So I make it clear right from the start, 'No X-rated stuff—I don't do that.' Or at least I try real hard not to. But sometimes stuff sneaks out. It's not my fault."

And so, through sad experience, cops come to learn caution when they follow a psychic into the backcountry of common sense, where deadly pitfalls and precipices abound for the unwary. Nowhere is the Boy Scout motto more appropriate: "Be prepared."

Yet, when it comes to getting more than is bargained for in psychic inquiries, it's not just the cops who are at risk, but the psychic as well. Call it a professional liability, but Amy is living proof of the ancient wisdom that when we cultivate our virtues we simultaneously cultivate our flaws.

About ten years ago, she was consulted on a break-in that occurred over in Manhattan. Dozens of Aztec relics had been stolen from an antiquities dealer. The thieves left no fingerprints, not a single trace.

That's when the dealer brought in Amy. He told her that, in making their getaway, the crooks had inadvertently dropped a bit of their loot. He hoped she might tune in to this item and help solve the case. Amy said sure.

The dealer handed her a six-inch sacrificial knife. It was made of the blackest obsidian and was very sharp. The dealer said, "Have at it."

So Amy lays hold on the handle and is immediately pierced by the image of a hill rising from the margin of a dark and tree-lined lake. Thousands of nondescript people are flocking to its summit, where an imposing temple looms over everything below. Directly in front of it is an altar, a huge greenish block of agate or jasper, its top side slightly convex, like the surface of a stony awesome eye. Behind it blazes a pair of ritual bonfires. The air is permeated with a vague stench, which brings to mind for Amy images of the house she grew up in behind the old Jack in the Box restaurant on South Livingston Avenue. Here's her swing set, there's her dollhouse, and now out of the blue appears her long lost collie dog, Laddie. She is aghast to see her own memories mingling with those coming off the grim artifact, as if the whole thing were just some informal cocktail party in the imagination.

Next she observes a half dozen priests emerging from the temple, each one wearing a long cotton robe adorned with hieroglyphic emblems of mystic import. Five of these priests are shrouded in black, whereas the sixth is mantled in scarlet and holds in his hands the very knife Amy holds in hers. As the procession draws closer, she can see that each priest's hair is matted with blood, the gory tresses flowing wildly over their shoulders. At the center of this gruesome pomp walks a naked and startlingly handsome young man. Given the circumstances, he's just a little too enthusiastic. He's waving to the crowd like a rock star.

When the grim procession arrives at the altar, the five black-robed priests stretch out the eager young man, face upward, upon the glossy surface of the stone. They secure his head and limbs. Now the scarlet-robed one lifts the black knife and holds its flinty tip just above the young man's chest. A deafening roar goes up from the crowd. This young man is definitely the star of the show. There's no going back. Even if he were in some way to falter, have a change of mind and cry out with all his might as the dark blade slits open his chest and a holy hand plunges into the gushing wound to tear out his palpitating heart, nobody could hear it anyway.

Well, maybe Amy could hear it—but she drops the knife at that critical moment and thereby draws the vision to a close.

Needless to say, she didn't solve this particular case, but the dealer was still pleased with her performance. It gave him a pretty good story to attach to an otherwise undistinguished relic, thus quadrupling its value in the marketplace. Combined with the insurance settlement on the lost goods, this meant he came out way ahead. He paid Amy double for her good work. When word got out about the knife, she started getting all kinds of calls from people wanting her to tell them if this sliver of wood they had came from the Cross, or this knuckle-bone came from Saint Peter and not, as those without faith would have it, from some barnyard pig. A professor who claimed to be an expert on the Shroud of Turin wrote a letter to the *Newark Star Ledger* demanding the Vatican grant Amy access to the relic, so the question of its authenticity might be settled once and for all.

Yes, Amy's business really took off, but nothing costs a person so much as something that is given, especially if by the gods. Imagine *not* having the power to forget, *not* being able to filter out the innumerable impressions that come via the senses and whatever other routes there are to perception, and instead, like Amy, possessing a Midas touch of memory. Everything you encountered then would immediately burst into image, thousands upon thousands of them, and you'd be swept up in a tornado of one thing turning into something else, an unbelievably violent flux in which nothing is ever fixed, no boundary ever secure. You'd be unable to distinguish between your own experience and that of somebody else—say, your butcher or the bastard who just cut you off in traffic—no longer able to know friend from foe, rich from poor, celebrity from nobody, false from true, weak from strong, foolish from wise, and—taking this where it must lead—one species from another. On and on it goes, until at last a terrible sameness cloaks the entire universe, so that not even the living and the dead can enjoy a blessed separation.

Loss of memory, we could conclude, might just be the greatest achievement of human consciousness. If only those flinty old senators from western states like Idaho and Utah had some sense of the fragility of the hard-won human ignorance in these matters, you could bet they'd be the first to demand the Clean Water Act be extended to include a certain River of Forgetfulness mentioned at the end of an ancient book, where all the disembodied souls about to be reincarnated are forced to drink a measure, that they might enter upon their new lives unencumbered by any clutter from the old.

Such is the nature of Amy's problem. Some say this is all just conjurer's shtick, but I don't know if it's that simple. After all, nobody is *required* to consult a fortune-teller, to obtain through prophecy or table rapping a treasure more easily acquired through prudence and down-to-earth discretion. No, when it comes to explaining why so many people in this day and age resort to palm readers, psychotherapists, and cult leaders, let's just say that nothing provides more comfort to a desperate person than to meet somebody who is even more desperate. This is not to impugn divination as an art, but only to note the pitiable hands into which it has fallen.

In Amy's defense, I would point out that her views about the weather coming off all things are compatible with those held by several ancient philosophers, most notably Anaximenes, who was the first to claim that the soul is made from air. Only a single sentence from his writings survives, but it's a lofty one: "As our soul, being air, both holds us together and controls us, so do breath and air encompass the whole cosmos." After all, we do say that the eyes are the windows of the soul, so it follows that the nose and mouth are the doorways. Thus, our psychological houses are more open to the elements than we think. No wonder human beings, even when they have nothing else in common, will find some way to talk about the weather.

I've heard Amy say that when we die our souls fly off to the moon. Once upon a time it was thought that all lost objects—not just souls but also garments, childhood toys, luggage, and wedding rings, as well as courage, virtue, beauty, and passion—found their way to the moon, where they reside to this day, hidden to all eyes save for those of the deity who reigns there. It may be that even one or two ideas have found their way there. All these lost things pass their time on the moon as if in sleep, which is yet another kind of weather, says

Amy, and they dream of their former existences back on the disburdening earth, flitting and fluttering around happy with themselves and
doing as they please. Until such time as the dream becomes so vivid
they wake up right where they belong, unable to tell if the whole
shebang were not itself just one big dream.

As for me, I am relieved that I am for the most part oblivious to
the things that cloud Amy's world. The weather around here affords
me enough clear days that I can keep track of the moon moving
swiftly through her phases, rather like the opening and closing of a
vast and sympathetic eye, at times full with remembrance, and at
others dark in a necessary fugue. Although nothing gives me greater
pleasure than to hear my friend Amy's stories and recount them to
others, I myself don't need to see the corpse candles and ghostly
beacons that, she assures me, hover over every object, no matter how
trivial.

Like I said, I tend to take her at her word.

THE GATED GATE

ON A NORTHERN CALIFORNIA HIGHWAY BEYOND THE WINE COUNTRY IS A sign for the Socrates Mine Road. What do you know! We were on the way to someplace else, but we wondered about the name and what the diggings looked like. It was worth investigating, so we turned onto the road, which was surprisingly wide and wended its way up the side of a scrubby mountain. It was a sunny afternoon in late May. No trees around here meant things would be getting pretty warm. On the crest of the ridge would be a cool forest, probably, but down here just an impenetrable medley of chaparral, one of the forms fire takes when not being fire.

You could tell at once this was no ordinary place. For all its sunlight, it seemed to be withholding something deep and close, almost familiar, leaving you with a sense that, despite your most earnest appeals, you would forever be kept in the dark. The chaparral shrubs were jammed together so fast they lost all individuality, as if in the thrall of some devil-and-everything obscurity. Here and there across the inhospitable slope, curious plumes of steam could be seen rising from earth into the sky. The landscape went on like this for a long time. We needed some relief.

Amid this steep vacancy we did pass a solitary ghost pine, its thin gray cloud of foliage offering little promise of shade. The branches sagged under a tremendous burden of cones—each the size of a schoolroom globe—which made it look as if somebody had come along and festooned the tree with a hundred ball-and-chains. We kept driving.

We didn't see any sign of the mine for a long time. Then came a little guard station with a gate that blocked further progress. An old man in a uniform came out and said that was it; beyond this was power company property, and we were not welcome. The uniform did not fit him very well, and he had a gun.

"We're looking for the Socrates Mine," we explained.

"Don't know nothin' about that," he said.

"Isn't this the Socrates Mine Road?"

"Yeah, but it's a stupid name."

"Well, how did it get that name?"

"Don't know. The only thing they mine around here anymore is steam to make electricity. Geothermal. Everything else is played out, and the steam's just about gone too. Every year there's less water. Now they have to pump sewage effluent into those wells just to keep things going. They haul it up here in big tanker trucks. Socrates Mine Road, my ass. Hot Shit Highway is what they oughta call it."

We turned around and left. When we got back to the highway, we had one last look at the sign that prompted our detour. A name, they used to say, is knowing.

The Socrates Mine Road.

GRAVE GOODS

IN THE YEARS JUST PRIOR TO WORLD WAR II, YOUNG GUS KENNY WAS studying philosophy at the University of California. He did not fare well in this department ruled by analytical philosophers, for he dearly loved to talk of the marvelous. In essays submitted to his professors, he found it pleasant to play poetically with the thoughts of the ancients. His mind moved in ways like the fogs that billowed in from the Golden Gate, shrouding the university in cold, gray obscurity. Unfortunately, then as now, this style of thinking is not much encouraged around university campuses.

Gus Kenny by temperament was one of those people who believe everything is connected to everything else—yet, he had a hard time demonstrating this to others, at least in a convincing fashion. In his investigations into the nature of things, he supplemented what he gathered from his five senses with wayward notions picked up from old books and the discourses of dead philosophers who came to visit him in dreams. He obtained some peculiar insights in this way, but most were lost. For instance, one night Charles Darwin showed up and presented him with a complete accounting for the mechanism behind natural selection. Evolutionary biologists would have regarded this bit of information as quite a boon, but the dreaming Gus Kenny never got an adequate handle on this or any other ghostly wisdom. When he awoke, the whole thing dissolved faster than autumn frost in morning sun.

For a couple years, the philosophy department suffered the irregular Gus Kenny, much as the village does its fool. It came to an abrupt end when he submitted his senior thesis. He was supposed to write a critical assessment of the philosophy of Nechepso-Petosiris; instead, he turned in a speculative reconstruction of the first map ever made by an ancient Greek to cover the entire known world. The original was drawn more than twenty-five hundred years ago by Anaximander, but nobody has seen it since. We only know about it because subsequent Greek writers made so much fun of it. "I laugh," writes one of them, "when I consider that many have drawn maps of the world, but no one has ever set it out in a reasonable manner." When Anaximander himself showed up one night in a dream to present Gus Kenny with the map, the old guy was still pretty bitter about the treatment he had received. Too bad for Gus Kenny his own efforts fared no better in the hands of critics.

A map? His professors demanded to know how *this* should count as philosophy. They were already in the habit of dismissing anything that didn't sound like Bertrand Russell, so from where they stood, Gus Kenny's project made no sense. For his part, the young scholar tried to get the professors to see the practical applications of his work. He explained that Anaximander was renowned for his ability to predict earthquakes, and this, according to Gus Kenny, had something to do with the map. It was a handy bit of lore, fanciful in its elegance. If nothing else such a map might have some use value, at least here in California.

Ah, but this was a university. Clarity was the only achievement these professors prized. They likened it unto a rare plant that grew only on the slopes of some faraway mountain, say Tamalpais across the bay. A life spent in diligent bushwhack up those steep slopes through impenetrable thickets of chaparral and hidden dens of snakes was hardly sufficient to catch even a glimpse of it. Granted, such methods seldom reveal a truth, but they do flush out gaunt syllogisms and tone the mind, which is all that counts. Oddly, none of these professors had ever actually been to Mount Tamalpais. No problem— when the weather was good they could see it from their office windows, so they felt comfortable using this metaphor.

After giving due consideration to the map, the professors warned Gus Kenny to give up philosophy. One of them described his thinking as "weedy." Another said it was "unbounded nonsense." Still another complained that this student had always been a lost cause, only now he has drawn a map to lead others astray. In the end, the professors rejected both map and Gus Kenny—they banished him from the groves of academe, or more precisely from the eucalyptus groves there at the foot of the Berkeley hills.

Committed nevertheless to his calling, Gus Kenny took his map and left the university, setting out in his solitary way to investigate philosophy. "Buddha, Socrates, and Christ," he reckoned, "when it comes to wisdom, the best stuff is from freelancers."

The world now lay before him, but he needed a job. He looked around for something that would pay the rent yet admit time to pursue his studies. As luck would have it, he found the perfect gig: a night watchman job across the bay in San Francisco.

⊕

In its day, Laurel Hill Cemetery was San Francisco's most prestigious burial ground. Along with the Masonic, Odd Fellows, and Calvary Cemeteries, it was part of a huge graveyard complex, locally referred to as the "Big Four." They spread around the base of Lone Mountain, like the severed arms of a stony-lonesome starfish cast up on a coastal hill. As the city swelled, its graveyard population grew apace, but over the course of time these melancholy neighborhoods suffered a decline in attention as vital interests moved elsewhere.

By the turn of the century, urban growth had transformed the graveyards into the geographical heart of San Francisco, a development municipal planners found worrisome. One of them publicly lamented the city was being "split in two by this death-dealing cemetery ridge, where every wind that blows carries anguish and desolation to some home." Land brokers jealously eyed the seventy square blocks of prime real estate now occupied by the dead, so in 1901 the city outlawed burials and the sale of cemetery plots within its boundaries. After that, the graveyards just went to hell.

Nevertheless, the Lone Mountain graveyards blossomed in the wake of human neglect. From the untended graves and rogue outcrops of serpentine, native vegetation burst forth in an effusion of grassland and soft chaparral. Beds of poppies, lupines, and buttercups sprang up across the abandoned acres, spreading far and wide a living light like the sunset sky. It was ideal habitat for bees, songbirds, and covert sweethearts. Even the tombstones went feral, taking cover among the rank growth along with all the other wildlife. Although in effect they constituted a vast city of the dead, these graveyards became—as far as plants and lovers were concerned—the last refuge of pristine California on the San Francisco Peninsula.

Yet, things wouldn't remain this way. Over the course of its history San Francisco, ever boastful of its lifestyle, has never been cordial toward death and its precincts. By the time of the gold rush, the city's oldest burial ground—Mission Delores—had already become a horrid block of unmade beds for the dead. The deceased, if they received any postmortem care at all, were placed in shallow sandy graves soon disclosed by wind. More often, the corpses were just tossed into the graveyard enclosure without ceremony, usually at night. A putrid stench gripped the neighborhood at all times, and citizens avoided passing anywhere near the place. People seen in the vicinity were presumed ghouls. Turkey vultures cut endless circles in the sky, and sheep grazed heedlessly across the grounds, nibbling on tufts of grass that popped up like blessed isles in a sea of old bones.

At the outskirts of town, unsanctioned burial grounds proliferated faster than fast food strips do today, but the city soon extended beyond even these far-flung boneyards. Commercial factions started demanding their removal. On February 7, 1853, the *Daily Alta California* ran a grisly story about a botched effort to relocate bodies from an informal North Beach graveyard to the new and "official" Yerba Buena Cemetery. The article reported that "the dead were disinterred without much regard, then pitched into heaps by the roadside, thence shoveled into carts and driven off. The coffins that were much decayed were burnt, but the sound ones sold for firewood." The new Yerba Buena Cemetery quickly reached capacity and was closed in 1861. The bodies once again were dug up, then relocated to Golden Gate Cemetery, which in turn filled to overflowing and was shut down in 1909. This time they didn't bother removing the bodies, only the tombstones. Today, at the Lincoln Park Golf Course on Legion of Honor Drive, you can tee off and play eighteen holes on top of all those forgotten California pioneers.

Every once in a while, however, they do come back to stir our memory. As in 1993, when, during a seismic retrofit of the Palace of the Legion of Honor, a few hundred of them were unearthed, a good many still wearing their vintage Levis. This unexpected resurrection generated excitement among a few archaeologists and historians, but it frustrated those who had bills to pay. The museum, for one, was obliged to cover steep surcharges for the delays caused by the discovery. "I suppose it's interesting," remarked one of its officials wearily, "but it's not exactly King Tut's tomb." On the other hand, genealogists of all kinds began making frantic inquiries. The manager of the firm handling the excavation grumbled, "We get imploring letters and faxes every day from people wondering if we'd found their great-grandfathers."

With all the moving around that goes on in the City by the Bay, it's sometimes difficult to distinguish the living from the dead. And as far as family trees go, you will sooner find your ancestors in heaven than anywhere in the San Francisco earth.

One by one, each graveyard in the city was excavated, evacuated, bulldozed, and built over. By World War I, only the "Big Four" remained, and these had reverted to an eerie prehuman landscape. To developers this represented a dark hole of wilderness in the otherwise bright urban universe. Coyote brush, coastal sage, and poison oak now choked the gravel paths. Over the course of time, tombstones had been toppled by earthquakes and vandals. Statuary, such as brooding angels and mournful Madonnas, had become bedraggled and weatherworn, their broken-off wings, arms, and legs strewn among wooly thickets abuzz with bees and cicadas. It was as though, in the presence of unruly nature, all human notions of death had dropped to the ground of exhaustion. Real estate agents and investors were appalled that Lone Mountain had been left to lie as such a waste. Something had to be done.

In California, where not even death and taxes are certain, the only thing to count on is development. Thus, it surprised no one when in 1914 Mayor "Sunny" Jim Rolph Jr. signed an ordinance to rid San Francisco of its remaining graveyards. He nevertheless offered a few words of explanation for what was about to happen. "No feeling is more honorable or creditable than respect for the dead," he intoned, "but the duty of government is more to the living than to the dead. We must provide for the expansion of our city. It must be a city of homes and not tombs."

He failed to anticipate just how difficult the dead can be to move. Public outcry over disturbing some of the city's most illustrious citizens from their eternal rest delayed relocation efforts for more than a quarter century. By the time the last of the bodies were evicted from their mournful tenements around Lone Mountain, the mayor himself had joined their company. Even so, the "Big Four" were finally erased, first from city supervisors' maps, then from the landscape itself. Laurel Hill Cemetery was the last to go.

⊸

The Laurel Hill Cemetery Removal Project got under way on the morning of February 26, 1940. Later that day, just as the sun was going down, Gus Kenny entered the graveyard through an old graystone gate on California Street and walked up along a narrow twisting lane toward an old gray-stone chapel. The cemetery grounds sloped upward in a dismal chaos of tombstones, obelisks, and vandalized vaults. Near the old chapel was a distinctive serpentine outcrop crowned with a thick and low-lying mat of shrubby vegetation, its spindly brown-red branches and narrow gray-green leaves flopping down in masses over the sides of the chrome-gray rock.

In the gloomy distance, Gus Kenny could see ancient cypress trees spreading their arms over disheveled graves and weary cemetery workers—day laborers, whose grim forms might easily have been taken for shades amid the deep cypress shade now handing over the hours to the still deeper shades of night. Just then, the five visible planets appeared together above the western horizon, hustling after the sun like some celestial clean-up crew.

As night watchman for the Laurel Hill Cemetery Removal Project, Gus Kenny took up his post in the old gray-stone chapel. The atmosphere was dank and musty. The pews and altar had long since been stripped out and hauled away. There was no electricity, no phone, no running water, and the roof leaked. The only furnishings were a rickety chair and a makeshift desk of old pine planks laid across a couple of wobbly sawhorses. An old kerosene lamp on the desk huffed out what light it could, along with dark clouds of smoke.

Gus Kenny had brought along a lunch box and his big book of Plato. Wearing a freshly pressed watchman's uniform, he sat down in the rickety chair at the pine-plank desk and began to fathom philosophy. All night long, while moths rattled at the dingy lamp, something could be heard scuttling around in the cellar below, something else fluttering in the rafters above. The next day, Gus Kenny brought the map given by Anaximander in a dream. He hung it up on the bare wall above the desk. Now his office was complete.

The night watchman was expected to guard against vandalism and malicious mischief. Over the years, Laurel Hill Cemetery had become a haven for grave robbers, pranksters, and horny teenagers. On foggy, moonless nights, shadowy apparitions could be seen flitting into and out of the decrepit mausoleums. From time to time, ominous clanks and moans resounded across the grim expanse of the graveyard. Such racket usually meant the gates of hell had been flung open; either that or some sledge-swinging ghoul was at it again, looting vaults for gold teeth, silver coffin handles, and bronze mortuary urns. Likewise, when mysterious flames leaped up on the dark ridgeline, it was either witches holding a black mass or the local high school students having another bonfire rally, feeding the blaze with old fence stakes pulled from grave borders.

Gus Kenny didn't bother to investigate any of these ordinary commotions. Not that he feared ghosts or ghouls, witches or jocks, but he was loath to abandon his studies. Every once in a while, he just stepped outside the door to perform a cursory inspection, as much to clear his lungs as to take a look. Nearby was an old crypt, nearly collapsed upon itself but still attended by a tottering piece of statuary, a nearly fallen guardian angel. This, he was told, had been the tomb of a famous nineteenth-century poet, but San Francisco's drastic graveyard ordinances so scared the family they had the body removed and cremated. The ashes were carried away to a safe and secret place, long since forgotten. The poet's name went there too.

Days and months passed. As more and more of the dead were grubbed out of Laurel Hill, Gus Kenny pursued his studies for the most part undisturbed. During the day, while he was sleeping in his rented room in the Sunset District, gangs of day laborers were fencing off sections of the old graveyard, digging up bodies, putting them in pine boxes, and shipping them out in trucks to Colma, south of the city, where they would eventually be reinterred in new earth.

Often the day laborers ran out of light and would have to leave a stack of loaded pine boxes just outside the chapel door. At first, Gus Kenny resented this intrusion, but after a while he grew fond of his moldering visitors. He found them companionable enough, and soon came to refer to them as his "darlings of the dirt." Propriety, however, kept him from delving too deeply into the dark privacy of their domain.

If he harbored any doubts about the unlikely place he was now seeking wisdom, they were laid to rest when he came across this passage in Plato's *Phaedo:* "Ordinary people are not likely to be aware that those who pursue philosophy aright study nothing but dying and being dead." After reading these words, Gus Kenny stood up from the rickety chair, walked to the chapel door, opened it, and looked out. The fog that night was so thick he couldn't see a thing. Ah, but his heart—perhaps it was due to all those rumpled graves out there— his heart was gripped by a certainty that shivered him all to pieces.

That's when it occurred to this college dropout—this reject from the philosophy department at the University of California—that the city of San Francisco, with all its ordinances against the dead, with all its haste to subdivide, multiply, and hide the truth, was in effect banning philosophy. How can you study and practice something that's kept hidden from you?

He went back into the gray-stone chapel and resumed his work, plunging ever deeper into the big book of Plato. Every now and then, he looked up through the lamp smoke at the outlandish map. Such was his routine, more or less, every night for the next sixteen months, which is how long it took the day laborers to remove the thirty-eight thousand bodies that lay in Laurel Hill.

⊕

The year 1940 passed in due course. For most of his time on the job, Gus Kenny didn't see a soul, but that didn't mean they weren't out there. One night shortly before the removal project got under way, a local biology teacher was caught in Laurel Hill with a gunnysack full of skulls. He said he wanted to stock the specimen cabinet in his classroom and put on a good display for the students. The idea had come to him a few days earlier while talking to a friend who regularly botanized in the graveyard.

"There's so much good stuff out here," he tried to explain to the authorities. "You can't just let it go to waste." They relieved him of his booty and let him off, but this kind of thing had to stop. That's when they decided they needed a night watchman.

Not long into the job, Gus Kenny was visited by the day watchman, a sluggish old man with skinny hands and oxidized complexion. His name was Pickthorn. Gus Kenny had been warned about him. Pickthorn was one of those old-timers whose memory had become a potter's field. Nothing gave him greater pleasure than to dig around there, preferably in front of a witness or two. Gus Kenny had some familiarity with this type of person, and he knew that reckless exhumation of one's psyche wasn't simply the mark of a dotard. He had friends his own age over in Berkeley who did the exact same thing; they called themselves artists.

That evening when Pickthorn appeared in the chapel, Gus Kenny looked up from his big book of Plato and saw this strange man's eyes glittering with intention. He knew what was about to happen— everything would go Ancient Mariner or maybe Flying Dutchman—so he just closed the big book with a sigh. "What brings you here at night, Pickthorn?"

The old man sat himself down on a stack of old boards and launched into a monologue. He didn't so much speak as pant out his words, a sour ghost hitched to every breath. It was the story of his life. The edited version goes something like this.

For more than sixty years Pickthorn had served as caretaker for the Laurel Hill Cemetery, the only job he had ever had. He would have stuck with it till the end, if the removal project hadn't forced his retrenchment. The planners felt bad about this, so they hired him on as day watchman. Small compensation, though, since the days on this job were numbered—when the bodies ran out in Laurel Hill, so would Pickthorn's luck.

Not a lot happens in the life of a graveyard caretaker. The same is true for most people. What does occur is neither interesting nor dull, save for in the telling. In accounting for himself, Pickthorn employed an abundance of wayward maxims: "A dead bee makes no honey." "Read a book, find a ghost; read a tombstone, lose your memory." "Where the Devil won't go, he sends in his grandmother." He intended these adages not as moral reflections but as histories of actual events he had participated in. It was as if the story of his life had been loaded into old boxcars of folk wisdom and superstition, then strung together into a phantom train and hauled down the tracks by an engine losing steam. Now poor Gus Kenny was caught at an isolated railroad crossing; all he could do was watch in quiet exasperation as the slow freight rolled by, no end in sight.

He worried that Pickthorn's presence in the chapel that evening was just the shadow of bleaker things to come—such as the old man showing up every night to disburden himself of his life's details. But as it turned out, Pickthorn did get everything off his chest—or at least as much as he needed to—because after taking his leave, some-time well after midnight, he went home to his caretaker's cottage at the far edge of Laurel Hill and quietly passed away in his sleep. The project supervisor stopped by the next night to give Gus Kenny the news.

"I pity those poor stiffs," the supervisor said, gesturing with his thumb toward the gouged-out graveyard. "Pickthorn's with them now. He had no family, so we took him down to Colma along with everybody else." These tidings gave Gus Kenny an unexpected chill. When the supervisor left, the young scholar returned to his big book of Plato with renewed attention. Months passed without further interruption.

Yet, by the end of August, his studies had not yielded the philo-sophical riches he had hoped. At that point, he was deep into Plato's dialogue called the *Ion*, all about the nature of poetry and its relation to knowledge. The piles of notes he had heaped up around his desk left him feeling at a loss. Compared to the work already accomplished by the day laborers, who in six months had made a significant dent— indeed, ten thousand of them—in Laurel Hill, Gus Kenny's progress in philosophy was paltry. Besides, all that tossing of cemetery earth had laid a pall of unwholesome staleness over the place. He tried not to breathe too deeply, but it left him feeling drowsy; he often dozed off now while reading, his head pillowed on the big book of Plato.

Most disappointing, though, was his languishing relationship to the other dead philosophers—they had stopped paying him visits in dreams. He worried they were jealous of the time he was devoting exclusively to Plato. On the other hand, he sometimes was able to find a way through sleep into the aviary of his own mind, where he watched delightful notions, swift and rare and lovely of wing, catching fire as they shot across the ceiling of heaven. In such moments, at least, Gus Kenny was truly a philosopher! But inevitably, upon rousing in the dim and smoky chapel, with a crick in his neck and his big book damp from drool, he was galled by the realization that the magnificent ideas flashing across the firmament of his dreams were, in waking life, no more distinguished than starlings around a block of suet. He needed a new approach.

Swearing off amateur bird-watching, he pledged himself to some rigorous ornithology. He laid aside the big book of Plato and turned to Aristotle's *Rhetoric,* only to discover—to his great dismay—Plato's most able student was adamant in demanding *clarity,* not wisdom, as the goal of philosophy, and worse, that the principal care of the philosopher was not for the soul but to avoid ambiguity at all costs. One passage was particularly troublesome. After urging his readers to adopt a transparent style of expression, Aristotle concludes: "Unless, indeed, you definitely desire to be ambiguous, as do those who really have nothing to say but pretend to mean something. Such people are apt to put these things into verse."

It was clear to Gus Kenny: Aristotle was the John J. Audubon of the mind, blasting exotic birds out of the sky in order to paint pictures of them more pleasing than anything actually found in the field. Something about it reminded him of his old professors back at Cal, who treated philosophy as if it were a cemetery removal project, and truth just one more Laurel Hill.

For a long time Gus Kenny stared down at the piles of notes around his desk, then, as if possessed by a mighty spirit, gathered up the papers, took them outside, and—with the tottering guardian angel looking on—deposited the whole lot in the vacant tomb of the unknown poet, just as the morning star made its appearance. That done, he returned to the gray-stone chapel for one last activity before ending his shift that night—he composed a poem.

It was the first of a series that in later years enjoyed some minor influence on the San Francisco poetry scene:

> *Black is some distraction*
> *as when day*
> *bends over*
>
> *white is reduced*
>
> *to a chute of stars*
> *on a moonless*
> *summer night*
>
> *Venus in a leotard*

Pleased with this, his inaugural effort in verse, Gus Kenny hung it up on the wall next to the map. Many more such lyrics would follow before the removal work was finished.

Near the end of October, the supervisor warned Gus Kenny to keep an especially close eye on the grounds. In previous years, problems arose when whole skeletons were disinterred and carried off for use as Halloween decorations. It was shocking. For days afterward, household dogs could be seen trotting around the adjoining neighborhoods with unspeakable treasures clamped between their jaws.

Gus Kenny swore his vigilance, but still dozed off, as always, for long stretches at a time, dreaming his book-induced dreams. Fortunately for all concerned, the night itself came to his aid—shortly after sunset, Saturn and Jupiter rose up over the eastern horizon like the orbs of some bug-eyed warden. Thus, while Gus Kenny dropped off from his watch into sleep, an inescapable surveillance was nonetheless maintained over the living and remaining dead in Laurel Hill.

✧

Near the one-year anniversary of his taking the watchman's job, Gus Kenny was studying philosophy in the usual way—chasing it in his dreams—when a loud knock on the chapel door startled him awake. It was after midnight. The last person to visit him on the job was Pickthorn, so it was without enthusiasm that Gus Kenny—smoke-huffing lamp in hand—went and opened the door. An old woman was standing there, holding a shovel and a gunnysack. Gus Kenny didn't like the look of this.

The old woman suddenly began to cough and took an abrupt step back, raising a gloved hand to cover her mouth and nose.

"Young man," he heard her say through a garden glove, "what is it you do in there?"

"Philosophy. I study philosophy. I used to go to Cal but—"

"Philosophy!" she exclaimed, dropping the hand from her face. "I thought you might have been the watchman. Well, then, you won't mind coming out into the fresh air on this fine clear night to help me with a small project."

"Forget it, lady. I won't stop you from playing the ghoul, but you're on your own." Gus Kenny was having a difficult time imagining what was left to rip off from Laurel Hill.

"A ghoul! Is that what you take me for? Listen up, young man, I'm not one of those better businessmen plundering Laurel Hill. Far be it from me to disturb the dead. I'm here to rescue a special plant—that one over there." She pointed toward the nearby hillside with its distinctive outcrop of serpentine. "Nobody will mind or even notice if I remove it. I'm going to transplant it. Now, come assist me—it won't take long. The moon is bright and full, so please leave behind that horrid lamp. Since you are a philosopher, you can share with me with some of your sayings."

She was already turned and walking away by the time Gus Kenny had figured out that he had no "sayings," unless he counted those of Pickthorn. Indeed, nobody had ever asked him for this kind of thing before. Perhaps the old woman was right. A philosopher—a genuine philosopher anyway—ought to have his own sayings, his little nuggets of wisdom to offer the general public. Otherwise what use is he?

Meanwhile, the old woman had reached the spot where the serpentine cropped out. By the light of the moon, Gus Kenny could see her lay aside the shovel and gunnysack, get down on hands and knees, and begin to inspect the tangled mat of vegetation that crowned the gray-chrome rock.

"Is that what you're here for?" he called over to her. "That ratty little bush? What are you, a gardener or something?"

She ignored him and continued her inspection. Then she stood up, took hold of the shovel, and began to dig.

Against his better judgment, Gus Kenny went over to investigate this matter more closely. He stood near enough to observe the old woman lifting small spadefuls of soil from around the shrub, but offered no assistance. He was still ruminating on his lack of sayings. Suddenly, the old woman scolded him.

"Don't be afraid of it, young man, it's only a manzanita. *Arctostaphylos franciscana.* Long ago it grew all over San Francisco on outcrops like this, but all those places have been built over. For the last fifty years, the only sites left to this poor species have been in the cemeteries around Lone Mountain. Now those too are gone. This particular shrub is the last one remaining in the wild. Nobody else seems to care about it, so I'm going to take it where it will suffer no harm."

"Where's that?" Gus Kenny asked.

The old woman again ignored him, and resumed her gentle work of shoveling the thin and stony earth from around the base of the plant, until its roots were fully exposed. The moonlight imbued the gray-chrome leaves and spindly red-brown branches with an eerie significance. It looked like the wedding veil for some wraith.

"All right, young man, now I require your assistance. If you would be so kind as to dislodge this shrub for me. I'm afraid I just don't have that kind of strength anymore."

To his own surprise, Gus Kenny complied. He squatted down, reached his hands under the branches, and wrapped them around the base of the shrub. Then he gave a stiff tug, and it all came loose with a sound something like a hundred mouse tails being snapped off all at once. As he stood up with the tangled mat in his arms, he felt—just for a moment—as if he were in possession of some long-lost shibboleth or magic word, its ancient meaning still clinging to the roots, along with clumps of fusty soil.

"Please place the *franciscana* in here."

She was holding open the gunnysack. Gus Kenny slipped the spindly shrub into it like a letter into its envelope.

At that very moment, a harrowing moan went up from one of the nearby mausoleums, followed by an exhilarated teenager's voice bouncing around among the tombstones: "Rock-a-bye baby, oh baby!"

Gus Kenny gave the old woman a sheepish look. "I suppose I should go break that up. It's my job."

"Young man, I thought you said you were a philosopher."

"I am. What do you mean?"

"Look around this place. Do you think all those monuments out there are for the dead? That all the tears ever spilled around these graves were for them? No, these markers are for the tens of thousands of forgotten nights of passion that incarnated all those souls in the first place. Each tombstone is an altar to lovemaking—and that's why the youngsters are drawn here. Graveyards are the temples of Aphrodite. Philosophers and their stern ways don't belong here."

With that, she hustled off down the lane toward the gray-stone gate, shovel in one hand, swelling gunnysack in the other, leaving behind a bewildered Gus Kenny, standing under a full moon in the not quite vacant graveyard.

Just before she slipped from sight, the old woman turned and called back: "Thank you for your help." He gave her an uncertain wave, then she was gone.

Gus Kenny decided not to look into anything else going on in Laurel Hill that night. Instead, he returned to the gray-stone chapel, wrote another poem, and hung it up among all the others around the map on the wall. Then he resumed where he had left off in the big book of Plato. Soon he was back chasing philosophy in the usual way, dreaming by smoky lamplight in an old graveyard as it was passing away.

❧

Four months later, the Laurel Hill Cemetery Removal Project came to a close. A few nights before his last scheduled duty as watchman, Gus Kenny fell asleep over the final pages of Plato's *Republic* and found himself in a dream-landscape Laurel Hill that stretched out to cover the entire city of San Francisco. In fact, there was no city, only a dimly lit expanse of peninsula honeycombed with desolation—no trees, no shrubs, no vegetation of any kind, just open, empty graves and sterile earth and old bones strewn everywhere. What little light there was appeared green and seemed to leak from deep within the graves themselves, oozing forth like pus from sores—a land so damned even the dead shunned it.

From atop Laurel Hill, a California golden bear suddenly emerged from one of the open graves. It was wearing a necklace of acorns. The golden bear began to walk down the wasted slope toward the vacant tomb of the unknown poet, where it stopped for a moment and seemed to look right at the dreaming Gus Kenny, who was standing in front of the gray-stone chapel. The golden bear then slipped through a dark opening in the shattered stone on the side of the crypt, disappearing from sight.

Acting in that foolish way of dreams and bad horror movies, Gus Kenny decided to check it out. He walked over to the crypt and stuck his head through the same dark opening. Inside he saw the golden bear lying on the spoiled earth of the tomb, holding between her huge paws a strange, shapeless bundle. She was gently licking away at it, each lap of her tongue adding a measure of form, until at last a tiny golden cub came into being. The little bear then turned its head toward Gus Kenny, smiled, and said: "Philosophy buries its undertakers."

The golden cub then burst into a glorious light, and the whole fiery swirl shot right through Gus Kenny's eyes and out the back of his dreaming head, to assume its rightful place high in the twinkling night sky. Thus the young scholar was awakened from his dream, the last—so far as anybody knows—ever to be had in a San Francisco graveyard.

When he walked out the door of the chapel to clear his head, there was Arcturus burning bright above the western horizon. He took it as an omen.

Only a few days remained on this watchman job, but Gus Kenny knew his time was already up, his work here done. He went back inside the gray-stone chapel, took down his map and poems, gathered up the big book of Plato, and headed out for the last time. He paid a final visit to the tomb of the unknown poet, cast a glance toward the now-bare serpentine outcrop, then walked down along the narrow, twisting lane toward the gray-stone gate, and passed through it out onto California Street and into the rest of his life.

For the time being, a ransacked Laurel Hill was left to lie at the very heart of San Francisco, like some forgotten epic poem on the nature of things. Before the bulldozers appeared to clear the way for real estate development, a world war intervened. Yet, by the end of the decade a bright new neighborhood of homes appeared where once stood only tombs. Gus Kenny, however, never saw any of this. He had gone off to the war and did not return.

Postscript

IT'S FUNNY HOW A TALE SUCH AS GUS KENNY'S GETS SAVED FROM THE graveyard of history. Had it not been for Dirk Grattan, all of it would have been lost.

Grattan was one of those minor figures from the 1950s poetry scene in San Francisco, known for publishing a little literary magazine called *Shouldered Oar*. Some years back while doing research on the writer Kenneth Rexroth, I came across a collection of Grattan's papers in a library. Other than a few items gleaned from old newspapers, everything I know about Gus Kenny must be credited to Grattan's painstaking investigation and laudable interpolations. After all, he was the one who, when just a teenager, happened upon a cache of Gus Kenny's poems in—of all places—an old crypt nearly collapsed upon itself in the soon-to-be-obliterated Laurel Hill Cemetery. That was during the war years in the early forties.

"Reading those poems is what really turned me on to poetry," he reminisced in a piece that appeared in *Shouldered Oar*. This essay coincided with the 1955 publication of Gus Kenny's collected poems, a slim volume titled *Grave Goods*. Along with the poems, Grattan discovered "this strange map that made no sense." The story behind that didn't come to light until years later, when Grattan ran into some drunk in a bar who claimed he used to be a philosophy professor and knew all about the map. As a literary historian myself, I admit all this sounds rather dubious. It certainly would be helpful if the map itself were available, but unfortunately it is nowhere to be found among the Grattan papers. When I asked the librarians about it, none of them knew anything.

On the positive side, the papers do provide a convincing account of how Dirk Grattan was able to track down some of the men with whom Gus Kenny served on the front over in Europe. They all spoke fondly of this man they called "the Philosopher." He shared with them his sayings, most of which he attributed to a mysterious figure known only as Pickthorn. The veterans recalled that during the particularly cold winter of 1944–1945, young Gus Kenny helped keep their spirits up, in a most unusual way. He had brought along with him a big book from which he read aloud to them on those long, cold nights. When he finished a page, he would carefully tear it from the book and lay it on a small fire around which they all huddled to keep warm. This little ritual greatly pleased the shivering men, as much in body as in soul, so when Gus Kenny went missing in action, his loss was deeply felt.

It's not surprising that a story such as his, and the poems written by this unusual man, should generate a literary stir when it all finally surfaced. Yet, by the 1960s interest in him had already waned, and today few people even know his name. You can still obtain a copy of his collected poems if you look around hard enough in used book-stores, but regrettably they weren't printed on high-quality paper, so it's rare to find one that doesn't crumble in your hands when you open it.

From what I have been able to learn, once upon a time there was a place where the general public could go to read one of Gus Kenny's poems. During the late fifties, Dirk Grattan raised money to inscribe one on a brass plaque and install it on a retaining wall in the new Laurel Hill Playground, close to the spot where—so far as he could recollect—the old crypt had stood where he found the cache of poems.

Last year I went to visit that playground, hoping to see the plaque for myself, but I was unable to locate it. Asking around, I finally found an older resident who told me the plaque had disappeared some years ago.

"There was a poem on it," he recalled, and he knew it by heart. To the best of his memory, it went something like this:

Under a crumbling
Quietly passing moon,
My life is ending,
My funeral is over—
I become one with you.

John P. O'Grady is the author of *Pilgrims to the Wild* (University of Utah Press, 1993), a study of American wilderness writers. His essays have appeared widely in publications such as *Terra Nova, The Quest, Common Boundary,* the *Trumpeter,* and *ISLE.* He is associate professor of English at Allegheny College in Meadville, Pennsylvania, where he teaches environmental writing and American literature.